A
MILLENNIUM
OF
PRAISE

A
MILLENNIUM
OF
PRAISE

BY
DAVID BROWNE

AMBASSADOR

Belfast Northern Ireland **Greenville** South Carolina

A MILLENNIUM OF PRAISE

© 1999 David Browne

ISBN 1 84030 062 0

Ambassador Publications
a division of
Ambassador Productions Ltd.
Providence House
16 Hillview Avenue,
Belfast, BT5 6JR
Northern Ireland

Emerald House
1 Chick Springs Road, Suite 203
Greenville,
South Carolina 29609, USA
www.emeraldhouse.com

Contents

CONTENTS

A MILLENNIUM OF PRAISE

INTRODUCTION

I have brought together in this publication, a selection of pen-portraits of various hymn writers, many of whom will be strangers to the reader but their sacred poetry may well be instantly recognised. This is very much a personal choice, but one which I believe will interest and even fascinate the reader. The scribes of well-known hymns are a motley crew - poets and preachers, housewives and teachers, politicians and doctors; the ordinary and the extraordinary; the humble and the eccentric!

I have long had an interest in biography and I combined this with a specific enquiry into the lives of the writers of sacred poetry. However the accumulation of original biographies created a greater curiosity and so annual holidays had to include visits to the location of places associated with many of our subjects! To my family, I here record my apologies!

The gathered information was imparted - in small doses - to the congregation of my local church when I was given the opportunity to lead the Sunday evening praise. I sincerely hope that a greater congregation will enjoy reading about the often unknown writers of many of our favourite hymns.

A Millennium Of Praise

We may well be able to sing from memory 'Abide with me' or 'I've wandered far away from God' but what do we know of the authors?

Reader, take a stroll through this gallery of pen-portraits, which are arranged in chronological order for continuity or for a selected look.

David G. Browne
Bangor
August 1999

A MILLENNIUM OF PRAISE

"Let's sing hymn number such and such"- it's so familiar in our worship - but it was not always so! There was a time when the congregation did not sing and when there were no hymn books to sing from. Of course the Old and New Testament Scripture records many occasions when psalms and hymns and spiritual songs were sung by the congregation, but from the days after the apostles till beyond the Middle Ages, such practice was removed from the people. The Roman practice of worship was sacerdotal - and the people were unnecessary even for singing!

The Middle Ages were better named the "Dark Ages" as learning was restricted to the few and the Bible was denied to the people. The light of the Gospel was almost extinguished but nevertheless there was a rich heritage of Latin verse that was Bible based and evangelical in character. Several hymns to be found in modern hymn-books are in fact translations of Medieval Latin!

Consider the hymns 'Jesus, the very thought of Thee' by Edward Caswall and 'Jesus, Thou joy of loving hearts' by Ray Palmer. Both these hymns were translated from Medieval manuscripts! It was

long believed that the author of the Latin original was French but
some maintain that the script evidences an English hand.

"Jesus, the very thought of Thee,
With sweetness fills my breast;
But sweeter far Thy face to see,
And in Thy presence rest."

Trans. Edward Caswall 1814-1878

"Jesus, Thou joy of loving hearts,
Thou Fount of life, Thou Light of men,
From the best bliss that earth imparts
We turn unfilled to Thee again."

Trans. Ray Palmer 1808-1887

Imagine that nearly a thousand years on, we are singing an
English translation of what was formerly sung as a Latin chant!

The transition from the monotonous choir chants of the early
centuries to the enthusiastic congregational singing of this century
was a slow process. The corruptions of the Medieval church and its
Latin practices did nothing to involve the ordinary people but rather
excluded and exploited them. Travelling preachers - or " religious
roundsmen" as one historian called them - presented a mixture of
news, myth and their version of stories from the Bible, sometimes
sung in ballad.

It was not until the days of John Wycliffe (1324-1384) and his
"Bible men" that the Word of God was told to the people in a clear
and unadulterated form. Because religion had become a form of
entertainment in some ways, Wycliffe voiced his condemnation
of the "novelty of song." He said that "Christ did not teach His
disciples to sing but to preach the Gospel!" Nevertheless it was his
"Bible men" who became itinerant preachers and evangelists in both
word and music; their singing of the Psalms in English was vital to
their ministry. They earned the name of "Lollards"- whether or not
the word derived from the German meaning "soft singers"- their
influence was dramatic.

The Scripture in song became more familiar in Britain and paraphrasing was practised by many. It was not until the 16th century that a Psalter appeared and a further 150 years before a hymn book was produced.

Whilst the credit must go to Martin Luther for introducing hymn singing to the church in the language of the people, his success in Germany did not have an impact in these islands till the days of Isaac Watts.

The notable efforts of Kethe and Rous, Tate and Brady and Bishop Ken have contributed a mixture of Psalms and Paraphrases and sacred poems to our current hymn books. They also illustrate the transition from Scripture in verse to the Hymn we are familiar with.

"THE REAL CRADLE OF ENGLISH HYMNS IS THE ENGLISH BIBLE. THE NEW-FOUND BIBLE SEEMED TO THE REFORMERS THE DIVINELY GIVEN WELL-SPRING OF PRAISE."

JOHN JULIAN, HYMNOLOGIST

Chapter One

MARTIN LUTHER
THE MONK WHO SHOOK THE WORLD

Martin Luther was born in Eisleben in 1483 and entered the monastery when he was twenty-two. A visit to Rome and the performance of Tetzel selling indulgences roused Luther to protest against the errors of the papacy. In October 1517 he nailed his Ninety-five Theses to the door of the church in Wittenberg and declared that the Pope had no power to forgive sins. His dependence upon the Scriptures encouraged him to strike a blow for truth that would literally shake the ecclesiastical and political world. He enraged the authorities by burning the papal order condemning his writings and he was summoned to defend himself at the Diet of Worms. When he refused to withdraw anything that he had written, he made the momentous statement: "Here I stand, I can do no other. So help me God."

Luther's achievement was to give the Bible to the German people in their own tongue in 1522. He exposed the heresy and error of Romanism and proclaimed the doctrine of Justification. He also oversaw the replacement of the Latin liturgy by giving praise back to the congregation.

He believed that music should be used in the service of Him who gave it and he maintained that music "is one of the most beautiful and noble gifts of God. It is the best solace to a man in sorrow; it quietens, quickens, and refreshes the heart." Thus he set about transcribing Medieval Latin hymns, psalms and liturgical chants as well as composing new texts of his own. John Calvin was to adopt a stricter code of practice and insisted that only the Psalms should be sung and only to the metrical tunes.

Luther established a small choir in Wittenberg and appointed an excellent singer, who became the choir master. In 1524 the first German hymnbook - a "Protestant Hymnal"- was published containing many of Luther's own hymns.

His method for preparing the hymns and the musical accompaniment was novel. He employed two musicians, whose task was to re-create tunes that he would hum to them or play on the flute, as some suggest! These tunes were a mixture of what he remembered from the miners' songs that he heard from his father and from chants he sang as a choirboy. No doubt the efforts played by this trio would sound very strange to us today!

His aim was to eliminate profane and worldly songs entirely. He asserted that "the devil has no need of all the good tunes for himself," and he just took them away from him! It was his belief that a positive way to annoy the devil was to praise God by singing a hymn! Very soon Luther's compositions were being sung in the streets, and sometimes without a full appreciation of the words. He was particularly concerned about the young generation and for their sake he declared "we must sing, preach, write and compose verse" and to use all forms of music.

Luther's hymns proved to be most effective missionaries of the Truth and his literary endeavour is one aspect of the Reformer's life and witness that has been overlooked by his many biographers. The English poet Coleridge asserted that "Luther did as much for the Reformation by his hymns as by his translation of the Bible." We would not agree with that extreme view but nevertheless Coleridge identified the enormous contribution made by Luther's compositions. Almost forty hymns are accredited to the reformer.

The 'Monk that shook the World' transformed public worship and we are still reaping the benefit of his action. His Battle Hymn of the Reformation 'A mighty fortress is our God', based on the 46th Psalm was sung in church, in the streets and on the field of battle.

> "A mighty fortress is our God,
> A bulwark never failing;
> Our Helper He, amid the flood
> Of mortal ills prevailing,
> For still our ancient foe
> Doth seek to work his woe;
> His craft and power are great,
> And, armed with cruel hate,
> On earth is not his equal."

MARTIN LUTHER 1483-1546

"PRAISING GOD IS ONE OF THE HIGHEST AND PUREST ACTS OF RELIGION."

THOMAS WATSON, PURITAN DIVINE

Chapter Two

WILLIAM KETHE & FRANCIS ROUS

FORGOTTEN WRITERS OF WELL REMEMBERED SONGS

Neither of the above names come to mind as being memorable or worthy of note, yet their efforts have bestowed incalculable blessings upon the church and to each is owed a tremendous debt of gratitude.

Kethe is believed to have been a native of Scotland and a friend of John Knox. In 1555 he is mentioned as an exile at Frankfurt, and two years later he was to be found in Geneva, which had become a home for the Puritan refugees fleeing persecution in the reign of Queen Mary. He seems to have been fulfilling the role of an ambassador for the exiles and he travelled to Basle, Strasbourg and Geneva. Whether he was one of those who remained in 1559 to complete the Bible and the Psalms is uncertain, but certainly Kethe's contributions to the Anglo-Geneva Psalter can be identified.

By 1561, Kethe had returned to England and had been installed as rector of Childe Okeford, near Blandford. He maintained an association with the parish for over thirty years but he took time out, between 1563 and 1569, to be with the Queen's forces and the Earl of Warwick at Newhaven and the North.

His superb versification of Psalm 100 was written for the tune by which it is still sung. It appeared in Daye's Psalter in England in 1560 and may well have been familiar to Elizabethan writers, such as Shakespeare! The Psalm was adopted into the Scottish Psalter of 1564 and later into the 1650 production.

"All people that on earth do dwell,
Sing to the Lord with cheerful voice;
Him serve with mirth, His praise forth tell,
Come ye before Him and rejoice.

Know that the Lord is God indeed;
Without our aid He did us make;
We are His flock, He doth us feed,
And for His sheep He doth us take."

WILLIAM KETHE DIED 1594

The "Old One-Hundreth" tune was written by Loius Bourgeois, a follower of John Calvin. He was cantor in Geneva and was entrusted with the task of providing music for the metrical Psalter. This work was spread over many years, interrupted when Bourgeois was thrown into prison for the crime of making "unauthorised alterations in well-known tunes!" It was the personal intervention of Calvin that secured his release but Bourgeois decided to leave Geneva as his attempts to introduce part-singing in public worship were not being encouraged.

Rous performed a similar role to Kethe but without leaving Britain. He was a native of Cornwall and served as the member of Parliament for Truro, a duty he exercised along with his profession as a lawyer. He was a member of the 'Long Parliament' and opposed the King and the Bishops. Appointed to the Westminster Assembly of Divines as a lay member, he was given the responsibility of examining candidates for the ministry. The Assembly had been called in 1643 with the desire for uniformity of worship in England and Scotland. One part of their deliberations was to prepare a Psalter.

WILLIAM KETHE & FRANCIS ROUS

The contributions of Rous met with the approval of the Commons but the Lords preferred the work of a William Barton. The Assembly revised Rous and in 1646 published "The Psalms of David In English Metre." However, the General Assembly of the Church of Scotland were unhappy and set up their own committee. They produced the 1650 Psalter, which is current today. The 23rd Psalm by Rous was found acceptable and it is his version which appears in both the English and Scottish Psalters.

> "The Lord's my shepherd, I'll not want.
> He makes me down to lie
> In pastures green: He leadeth me
> The quiet waters by.
>
> My soul He doth restore again;
> And me to walk doth make
> Within the paths of righteousness,
> Even for His own name's sake."

The 23rd is the most loved and most familiar of the Psalms; its phrases are as well-known as the Scripture itself. The very words "the Lord is my shepherd" can be repeated and sung meaningfully as a personal testimony. Dr John Ker says that every word of the Psalm "every line of it, has accompanied from childhood to old age, has been to a multitude the rod and staff of which it speaks, to guide in dark valleys and at last through the darkest."

Another said that it is often the first religious verse to be learned at the mother's knee and the last to be repeated before entering "the valley of the shadow of death."

Rous was described as a veteran of many Puritan struggles and was given various appointments under Oliver Cromwell. He was made Provost of Eton College and was elected Speaker of Parliament. Cromwell further honoured him with a knighthood and in 1657 he was elevated to the House of Lords.

He died in his eightieth year, leaving his testimony in his will; it closes with these words:- "I lay hold of the free grace of God in His Beloved Son, as my only title to eternity, being confident that by the precious blood of His Son to present me faultless before the presence of God's Glory with joy."

He well knew the meaning of the third verse of the 23rd Psalm:-

"Yea, though I walk in death's dark vale,
Yet will I fear none ill:
For Thou art with me; and Thy rod
And staff me comfort still.

Goodness and mercy all my life
Shall surely follow me:
And in God's house for evermore
My dwelling-place shall be."

FRANCIS ROUS 1579-1659

"DYING TO SELF IS A PROGRESSIVE JOURNEY AND I HAVE COME TO BELIEVE THAT IT IS TRAVELLED ONLY THROUGH PRAISE."

MERLIN R. CAROTHERS, NORTH AMERICAN ARMY CHAPLAIN

Chapter Three

TATE & BRADY

REVISERS OF THE PSALMS

The names of Nahum Tate and Nicholas Brady are linked together for their ambitious seventeenth century project to revise the Psalms for public singing in worship. Their friendship prospered from similar backgrounds and with similar religious convictions and was to bring them to the Court of King William III. Both were accomplished writers, Tate was a playwright and Brady a preacher.

The reader will be familiar with the words of 'While shepherds watched their flocks by night' which came from the pen of Mr Tate. He distinguished himself as a man of rare talent but felt restricted by the literary environment in Dublin at the time of the Restoration. Thus we find him in London endeavouring to make his fortune. This was a disappointment to his father, Rev Faithful Tate, who had anticipated that his son, when he had completed his training at Trinity College, would follow him into the church.

The public's attention was drawn to Nahum by his talent in poetry and drama. He was the first poet to praise Britain's national drink in an ode called 'Panacea - a Poem upon Tea!' His speciality was adapting Elizabethan plays, particularly those of Shakespeare.

His reworking of 'Richard II' was given the title 'Sicilian Usurper'. However its run lasted only three performances as it was taken off stage because King Charles decided that the political parallels were too explicit!

Tate numbered among his friends the poet John Dryden, the composer Henry Purcell and the influential Earl of Dorset. The latter became his patron and a well placed word in the ear of King William secured his appointment as Poet Laureate in 1692. With the position came an annual sum of £100 and gave him opportunity to join Brady in revising the Psalms. Their 'New Version' was dedicated to the King and was published with royal approval in 1696. The effort had the lukewarm endorsement - "permitted to be used in all churches as shall think fit to receive them." The remark was more perceptive than they realised and their production was largely unsuccessful. The novelty of their work was soon overtaken by the similar efforts of others and the only surviving revision is 'Through all the changing scenes of life', based on Psalm 34.

His colleague Brady was a popular preacher, poet and author. At the time of their association he was chaplain to King William III. He too had graduated from Trinity College in Dublin and his vocation took him to Cork where he became Prebendary. He was a native of Bandon, which is not far from Cork. He espoused the cause of William and under his leadership the people of Bandon rallied together to repel successive attacks by the forces of King James to destroy the town. His gallantry was applauded and he was recommended to receive a Doctorate of Divinity from Dublin University for "services rendered to the Protestant Cause."

The citizens of Bandon and supporters in Cork resolved to dispatch him to London with a petition of loyalty to King William. To their loss he remained in London, where his style of preaching was much appreciated and resulted in the presentation of the charge of St Catherine's, the royal chaplaincy and later the incumbency of Richmond in Surrey, a position he held for thirty years. He also found time to organise a school at Richmond and to publish several volumes of sermons and a translation of Virgil's Aeniid.

Brady led a full and profitable life to the very end whereas Tate's latter years were spent in abject poverty, the fortune he had sought as a young man eluding him. Tate eventually had to seek shelter in the Royal Mint at Southwark, where debtors were protected from arrest. It was there that he died in July 1715. Brady survived him by eleven years.

"While shepherds watched their flocks by night,
All seated on the ground,
The angel of the Lord came down,
 And glory shone around."

NAHUM TATE 1652-1715

"Through all the changing scenes of life,
In trouble and in joy,
The praises of my God shall still
My heart and tongue employ."

NICHOLAS BRADY 1659-1726 & NAHUM TATE

"THE CHRISTIAN FAITH IS A SINGING FAITH. IN FACT, FROM THE BEGINNING TO THE END OF THE BIBLE, YOU WILL FIND SONGS OF PRAISE TO GOD. THIS PATTERN OF PRAISE HAS CONTINUED THROUGHOUT CHURCH HISTORY."

WARREN W WIERSBE

Chapter Four

THOMAS KEN
ROYAL CHAPLAIN AND ROYAL PRISONER

homas Ken, far from being an ordinary individual, lived an
eventful and extraordinary life - some would say he was an
eccentric. He became the friend and foe of successive
monarchs, at one time an honourable member at Court and at
another a prisoner in the Tower of London! He was noted throughout his life as a man of principle, with strong but sincerely held
opinions. Lord Macaulay, the historian, wrote of him: "His moral
character seems to approach as near as human infirmity permits to
the ideal perfection of Christian virtue."

Orphaned early in life, he was brought up by his sister Ann, who
had married Isaac Walton, the author of the classic "Compleat
Angler." It was in Walton's library that Ken became familiar with
Puritan writers, of whom Richard Sibbes was his favourite. His
privileged position and advanced education gained for him a teaching post at Winchester School. There he published "a Manual of
Prayers for use of the Scholars." Some of his hymns were to be
found in this work; these were not just poems to be recited or prayers
to be hastily mumbled but pieces to be sung.

Thus Ken can be credited with being the first to introduce hymn-singing to the English church. He progressed to Oxford University and was later appointed rector of a couple of parishes.

In 1679 he was elevated to be a chaplain at the Hague to Princess Mary, after her marriage to William, Prince of Orange. However the post was short lived because of his outspoken criticism of palace behaviour, and he returned to England. He then performed a similar role at the Court of Charles the second. When the king visited Winchester in 1683 and requested the use of Ken's house to accommodate his mistress, Nell Gwynne, Ken defied his monarch and rebuked his scandalous immorality.

Two years later Ken was surprised and delighted to be appointed Bishop of Bath and Wells by the same King Charles who at least recognised a godly man and respected him for daring to tell the truth!

The following ruler James II was not so accommodating to Ken's vocal denunciations and had him imprisoned in 1688. Ken had condemned the King's popish ways and with six other bishops, refused to read the Declaration of Indulgence. The seven bishops were locked up in the Tower of London and then brought before the Court of the King's Bench. To the king's consternation the seven were found not guilty of sedition and were released - coincidentally on the same day that a formal invite was extended to Prince William of Orange to deliver the nation from popish despotism.

Ken, because of previous animosity, would not welcome the Protestant champion, and he also declined to acknowledge Mary as Queen. He refused to take the Oath of Allegiance and this placed his bishopric in jeopardy. The Royal House put up with the awkwardness for a while but patience ran out and in 1691 he was deprived of office. He spent the remainder of his days in retirement, failing to be reconciled to either William or Mary, but outliving them both.

His death came in 1711 and he left strict instructions concerning the arrangements for his funeral and burial. He was to be buried in Frome church, "early in the morning, as the sun rises" and his hymn 'Awake My Soul' was to be sung. His wishes were fulfilled. Notice the fifth verse of his preferred funeral hymn, it includes the line 'Sing high praise to the Eternal King.' Surely mortal kings had earned his displeasure but only the Eternal King was worthy of Ken's praise.

The final verse must be the best known verse in English literature, often sung alone but also tacked on to innumerable long-metre hymns:

"Praise God from whom all blessings flow;
Praise Him, all creatures here below;
Praise Him above, ye heavenly host;
Praise Father, Son and Holy Ghost."

THOMAS KEN 1637-1711

"THE FIRST RECORDED HYMN IN THE BIBLE IS THE UTTERANCE OF THE THANKSGIVING OF ISRAEL AT THE RED SEA. WHEN THE CHURCH BECOMES VISIBLE, HER VOICE BECOMES AUDIBLE!"

ANONYMOUS

Chapter Five

ISSAC WATTS

THE FATHER OF ENGLISH HYMNODY

I n his mature years Isaac Watts was a grotesque figure to behold;
he was about five feet in height, bent over and his head seemed
too large for his body. Frail in health he found that his condition
improved when he took up residence with Sir Thomas and Lady
Abney. (Sir Thomas had been mayor of London and Watts was his
chaplain.) In fact he spent the last thirty-six years of his life there!
Watts was an unusual man, an expert in many fields of science and
philosophy, a writer on many complex subjects and also in simple
verse. He wrote textbooks on logic, papers on psychology, treatises
on theology and he published the first ever hymnal for children-
"Divine Songs for Children."

As a child he demonstrated a remarkable passion for learning.
At the age of 4 his father was teaching him Latin, and two years
later he was at Latin school and able to write; Greek was on the
curriculum in his ninth year and then French was added. He had to
wait another two years before he could handle Hebrew! It must be
stated that although he was an exceptional child he had a tender
heart and a humble nature.

In these formative years Nonconformist preachers were enduring persecution and imprisonment. His father had been locked up for his religious beliefs and as a baby Watts had been brought by his mother to keep vigil outside the prison in Southampton. He could later write his own testimony 'I'm not ashamed to own my Lord or defend His cause'. Well grounded in the Scriptures and well taught in the Catechism, he was much prayed for that he would early find the Saviour. At 14 he came under conviction of sin and the following year he recorded his conversion. He felt the call of God to enter the ministry, but his adherence to Protestant Dissenting views forfeited a university education.

In 1690 - a memorable year for many reasons! - Watts left Southampton to begin four years of training at the Nonconformists academy at Newington Green in London. The course completed he returned home but for a prolonged time remained in study- it seemed that there was a special task to prepare for.

At this time he associated with the local Independent congregation where his father was a deacon. One aspect of the services grieved him and that was the singing. His father suggested that he should produce something better, rather than complain! He did and every Sunday for the next two years he submitted a new item for praise. This was the basis for his collection of 210 hymns which he gathered in 1707 for the first real hymn-book in the English language, 'Hymns and Spiritual Songs'.

Watts commented that "while we sing the praises of God in his Church, we are employed in that part of worship which is nearest akin to Heaven, and it is a pity that this should be performed the worst upon earth!" He argued that in the use of the Psalms, only Old Testament themes were sung among New Covenant people. What was required was Psalms to be translated in such a manner "as to believe that David would have composed them if he lived in our day." He went on to produce "The Psalms of David Imitated in the Language of the New Testament" in 1719.

He was also critical of the practice of "lining out" which disjointed and disrupted the theme of the Psalm. This was the accepted singing method of the day; the song leader or cantor would read or sing one line at a time of the Psalm, which would then be sung by the congregation one line at a time! Thus a long Psalm would become a tedious effort to complete in song, and the whole sense of the message lost! Watts' new way was referred to as "regular singing." He thus made the Christian hymn part of modern worship. Things would never be the same!

Consider the rich legacy of paraphrases that Watts has left us: 'Jesus shall reign' based on Psalm 72. This was one of the earliest missionary hymns, yet written prior to the days of evangelical missionary endeavour! From Psalm 98 he wrote 'Joy to the World', an advent hymn, which he originally entitled 'The Messiah's Coming and Kingdom'. 'Our God, our help in ages past' was altered by John Wesley to be sung as 'O God, our help' and has remained so to this day. It has become Ulster's Protestant Anthem and rightly so as it echoes the thoughts of Psalm 90.

Among his hymns proper are 'Am I a soldier of the Cross', 'There is a land of pure delight', 'I'm not ashamed to own my Lord' and 'When I survey the wondrous Cross'. This latter hymn is, in the estimation of many, his supreme composition. It appeared in the 1707 edition of "Hymns and Spiritual Songs" bearing the title "Crucifixion to the world by the Cross of Christ- Galatians 6 v 14." It was his intention that the piece be sung at the remembrance of the Lord's Supper. The poet Matthew Arnold thought the hymn to be the finest in the English language.

In some respects Watts' career as pastor of Mark Lane Chapel and his theological writings have been overshadowed by his poetry, though he disclaimed any title to be a poet. He said "I make no such pretences in an age wherein so many superior souls shine." His written works had an extensive circulation - his "Hymns and Spiritual Songs" ran to sixteen editions during his life - and both Edinburgh and Aberdeen Universities bestowed doctoral degrees for his literary and academic achievements. He also prepared the plan for "The Rise and Progress of Religion in the Soul" but growing infirmity prevented him from writing it and he handed the work to Philip Doddridge, whose name was subsequently attached to it.

The dying divine said "If God has no more service for me to do - I am ready. It is a great mercy to me that I have no manner or fear or dread of death; I could, if God please, lay my head back and die without alarm this afternoon."

"When I survey the wondrous cross,
On which the Prince of Glory died,
My richest gain I count but loss,
And pour contempt on all my pride.

Forbid it, Lord, that I should boast
Save in the death of Christ my God:
All the vain things that charm me most,
I sacrifice them to His blood.

Were the whole realm of nature mine,
That were an offering far too small;
Love so amazing, so divine,
Demands my soul, my life, my all."

ISAAC WATTS 1674-1748

"TO WATTS MORE THAN TO ANY OTHER MAN IS DUE THE TRIUMPH OF THE HYMN IN ENGLISH WORSHIP. ALL LATER HYMN-WRITERS, EVEN WHEN THEY EXCEL HIM, ARE HIS DEBTORS. WATTS WAS A PIONEER."

BERNARD L MANNING, CAMBRIDGE SCHOLAR

Chapter Six

EDWARD PERRONET

ASSOCIATE OF WESLEY AND OTHERS

The Perronets were a Huguenot family, originally from Switzerland. They had fled persecution in the late 16th century and came to England where they could exercise their Protestant principles. In the mid-1700's Vincent Perronet and his son Edward were associated with the Wesleys and the Methodist movement. Charles Wesley referred to Vincent as the "Archbishop of Methodism," because of his articulate defence of their doctrine and discipline. Edward was John Wesley's companion on a visit to the North of England in 1749.

Wesley's Journal records this occasion and particularly the reception they had in Bolton. Opponents of their preaching seized Edward and proceeded to roll him in the mud and mire. The mob also attacked the place where they were lodging. Undaunted they ventured on to more exploits, Edward interpreting the experience as his introduction to serve Christ as an itinerant preacher. John Wesley ordained Perronet and was desirous to hear his young colleague preach but Perronet was determined not to preach before him. To force the situation Wesley announced publicly that the following day Perronet would indeed be the preacher. He was thus obliged to comply, but he suspected that Wesley would be present, even though he was aware of Perronet's reluctance.

At the announced time and venue, Perronet arrived and came to address the assembled congregation: "I am compelled by the request I have from Mr Wesley to occupy this place. I am entirely inadequate to the task; but, for all that, I will give you the best sermon that has ever been delivered." Had sinful pride overcome him, or had the occasion overwhelmed him, or had some super-natural power possessed him? No, none of these - because he read out the Sermon on the Mount and concluded the service! Wesley did not admit to being present, but he would now be mindful of the strong will of his novice!

Differences of opinion did arise with the publication in 1757 of a religious satire entitled "The Mitre." In this poem Perronet attacked the abuses of the Anglican church in a manner that aroused Charles Wesley's anger. The writing was "suppressed" but a breach was opened. He was forbidden to sell further copies, so instead he gave them away freely! Perronet maintained that there must be separation from the Church of England but Wesley would not agree. Then the licensing of itinerant preachers became a contentious matter. Although Wesley had ordained him, changing circumstances dictated a different approach.

By 1771 Perronet was convinced that he could not cooperate with the Wesleys any longer and he attached himself to the Countess of Huntingdon, under whose patronage he became Pastor of a chapel in Canterbury.

She in turn was unable to tolerate his vitriolic language against the Anglicans. Perronet resolved the situation by withdrawing from her support but took up the charge of an independent church in the same town!

He remained there till his death in January 1792. Ironically he was buried in the cloisters of Canterbury Cathedral.

Perronet's 'All hail the power of Jesu's Name' appeared in the "Gospel Magazine" for 1780, having previously been published in leaflet form. He had written a number of poems and hymns but none of them displayed much poetical talent. The rich scriptural allusion made this piece different. The original eight verses have been trimmed to five, and the sixth verse, which appears in most compilations, was added by John Rippon (1751-1836), one of C H Spurgeon's predecessors in New Park Street.

The hymn is usually sung to the tune 'Miles Lane' by William Shrubsole. He was just 20 when he composed the tune and he went on to become the appointed organist at Bangor Cathedral in Wales. However he was sacked from this position because his sympathies were evangelical. Perronet appreciated his friendship and left him a large sum of money in his will. This hymn is enthusiastically sung by all denominations, even in the Anglican church!

"All hail, the power of Jesu's Name!
Let angels prostrate fall;
Bring forth the royal diadem
And crown Him Lord of all."

EDWARD PERRONET 1726-1792

"THE MERITS OF A HYMN LIE CHIEFLY IN THE TUNE; THE EDITOR WHO WOULD DIVORCE OLD WORDS FROM THEIR ACCUSTOMED SETTING, IS AN ICONOCLAST OF THE WORST ORDER."

LORD BALFOUR, POLITICIAN

Chapter Seven

ROBERT ROBINSON
A SERMON THAT LASTED THREE YEARS!

R obert Robinson was born in Swaffham in Norfolk, into a family of "lowly parentage." Early in his life his father died and his widowed mother was left in severe straits. She bore a godly testimony in the face of pitiful circumstances and determined to do the best for her son. She held an ambition that he would become an Anglican minister and during his young years he heard this desire expressed over and over again. However his mother's wish did not coincide with his own plans!

Their financial plight dictated that after a few years of education, he should secure an apprenticeship. So at the age of 15, he left home to begin his career - in a barber's shop in London. This employment was neither interesting nor successful as young Robinson much preferred to have his head stuck in a book rather than attend to the clients. His distraction was often rebuked but he failed to learn a lesson. The solution was found when his employer pitched him out into the street, to fend for himself.

Freed from parental and an employer's control, Robinson thought he was now his own master and like the Prodigal Son he sought out friends of similar outlook to waste away both time and substance. On one escapade the gang attended a fortune-teller and to make things more interesting they paid for the encounter with alcohol. Filled with this "unclean spirit" the savant gave her predictions. Robinson was alarmed at her comments and fled in a state of fear. He resolved to subdue his youthful energies and to live a serious life. He abandoned his new friends and sought company in his books. These efforts at self-reformation satisfied his conscience but failed to meet the true need in his life.

When George Whitefield visited London, Robinson considered that he could well benefit from hearing the great preacher. The sermon that he heard was a message on Matthew 3 v 7 - "Who hath warned you to flee from the wrath to come?" For the second time he was overwhelmed with fear and the prospect of a future without Christ and without hope. The sermon was recalled again and again and the chastening was to last three years! In his twentieth year he found "peace in believing." He remained in London until 1758 and attended the ministry of Gill, Wesley and others. The time must have been well spent and his "new apprenticeship" completed for by 1760 he was preaching in various churches, including a Calvinistic Methodist chapel in Norfolk, an Independent (Congregational) work in Norwich and a Baptist church at Cambridge. The invitation to preach became a call to take full charge at the Baptist assembly. There he combined pastoral responsibilities with scholarly writing and he published two significant treatises - "A plea for the Divinity of our Lord Jesus Christ" and "The history and mystery of Good Friday."

His literary work attracted some interest and approaches were made to him to forsake his church and to join with the Anglicans. His mother's hope was not to be fulfilled as Robinson repudiated this invite and maintained his Baptist pastorate to his last days.

'Come Thou Fount of every blessing' was written at the beginning of his preaching ministry. Some have drawn attention to the third verse and the lines "Prone to wander, Lord, I feel it, prone to leave the God I love," as evidence of some spiritual instability. But is this not rather an expression of the necessity to depend upon, and a sincere plea for, close communion with the Lord - considering the imperfect state of man, this side of Eternity? Another of his hymns in common use is 'Mighty God, while angels bless Thee'.

Robinson's hymns have well been described as being "terse and yet rich but without sentimentality,"- something like his own personality!

Robinson retired in 1790, worn out from his diligent ministry of thirty years. Within weeks he had passed away, to arrive at Heaven's Home.

"Come, Thou Fount of every blessing,
Tune my heart to sing Thy grace;
Streams of mercy, never ceasing,
Call for songs of loudest praise.
Teach me some melodious measure,
Sung by flaming tongues above;
O the vast, the boundless treasure
Of my Lord's unchanging love."

ROBERT ROBINSON 1735-1790

"SINGING DOES AT LEAST AS MUCH AS PREACHING TO IMPRESS THE WORD OF GOD UPON PEOPLE'S MINDS. EVER SINCE GOD FIRST CALLED ME, THE IMPORTANCE OF PRAISE EXPRESSED IN SONG HAS GROWN UPON ME."

D L MOODY, EVANGELIST

Chapter Eight

SAMUEL MEDLEY
FROM SAILING THE SEAS TO SAVING SOULS

S amuel Medley was born in Cheshunt, Herefordshire, of godly
parents and grandparents. His grandfather, who was a school
master, was to play a significant role in his life. Samuel had
a devoted teacher and was given an excellent education. When he
embarked on an apprenticeship in the cloth trade, his grandfather
believed that he had not exercised his full potential but kept his
counsel and did not express his concern. The career was not a
success and an alternative had to be sought. The opportunity was
presented for young Medley to serve out his years of apprenticeship
in the navy and he grabbed the offer.

So at the age of seventeen he set sail with an ambition to be a sea
captain if not a commander! The tough life and rough pleasures
soon removed any thought of serious things and any lessons learned
in his Christian upbringing were forgotten. The tender heart of youth
changed into a heart of stone. He was totally unmoved at the sight
of his colleagues, many of his own age, being brutally killed by
cannon fire in a sea battle (Battle of Cape Lagos 1759). It is
recorded that the bloodshed was so great that barrels of flour were

tipped over the decks to staunch the blood and to prevent the men from slipping into the sea.

However, when it was his turn to suffer an injury and amputation of his leg was threatened, he began to consider his misspent life and to contemplate eternity. Although the wound was serious surgery was avoided and the leg began to heal; at the same time with danger ebbing his religious feelings began to subside. The navy had not much use for a lame sailor and he was dispatched to the home of his grandfather to convalesce.

The godly old man dutifully cared for his physical and spiritual needs. Medley appreciated the former but detested the latter. His discomfort was increased and full advantage was taken of his immobile condition when one of Isaac Watt's sermons on Isaiah 42 v 6-7, was read to him!

The Spirit of God began to apply the Word and Medley realised his blindness, his imprisonment and his darkness. Reader take a look at those verses for yourself! The date was July 5th, 1760 and he recorded that he received peace and pardon through believing and claimed Christ as the captain of his salvation.

The change in his life was dramatic and any notions of a naval career disappeared. He refused to let his disability hinder him and he arranged for porters to take him to hear the great preachers of the day, like George Whitefield and Andrew Gifford. Unable to do a day's work, he spent his time studying Hebrew and Greek and of course the Bible. As his physical frame had strenghtened he used his knowledge to commence a school in London. Not only that, but his ability at preaching was recognised and this led to him becoming a pastor in the Particular Baptist church.

By 1779 he was pastoring in Liverpool where the congregation had dwindled to about a dozen. Soon the work expanded and a new building was required to accommodate the people. His sermons were laced with vivid stories of the sea and these undoubtedly were instrumental in striking a chord in the heart of many a sea-faring man. He taught his flock hymns of his own composition and these were distributed in leaflet form. It was the practice then for the hymn to be recited a line or two at a time, and then sung in couplets! His method ensured uninterrupted singing. He was able to touch many souls with his hymns, which were full of Christ and the riches of his grace. One old preacher expressed his appreciation thus: "he always lands you in heaven in the last verse!"

This is certainly true of his 'Now in a song of grateful praise'. Medley died in 1799 at the age of 61. His dying testimony was that "the Jesus whom I have so long recommended to poor sinners is my only comfort in my dying hours. I die no Arminian - I die a poor sinner saved by sovereign, rich and free mercy." His last uttered words were "Glory! Home - home!"

"Now in a song of grateful praise
To Thee, O Lord, my voice I'll raise;
With all Thy saints I'll join to tell:
My Jesus hath done all things well."

SAMUEL MEDLEY 1738-1799.

"WE THANK GOD THAT SO MANY OF OUR HYMNS ARE SOLID IN THE THEOLOGY THEY BREATHE, AND SO MANY OF THEM HAVE BEEN EXPRESSLY USED OF GOD IN THE CONVERSION OF MEN AND WOMEN TO THE SAVIOUR."

REV WILLIAM CLARK, PREACHER & AUTHOR

Chapter Nine

THOMAS KELLY
AN IRISH SEPARATIST

The Cross of Christ - what a wonderful theme - and one taken up by Thomas Kelly in several of his hymns. His sacred poem 'We sing the praise of Him who died' was well described by Lord Selborne as a hymn that was "distinguished by a calm and subdued power." Kelly was adept at stating simple truths while dealing with essential and profound doctrines. His first collection of ninety-six items was published in Dublin in 1815 but eventually a total of over 700 pieces flowed from his prolific pen.

However, not all his compositions were totally original:- the words and theme of 'The Head that once was crowned with thorns', based on Hebrews 2 verse 10, were borrowed from John Bunyan's hymn of the same title!

Thomas Kelly was born the son of a distinguished judge, in Kellyville, Athy in the south of Ireland. He completed his education at Trinity, after which he entered at the Temple in London with the intention of practising law. He spent some time living in the capital where he befriended the celebrated Edmund Burke. However neither his friendships nor parental influence had a part in his change of career. He had begun to study Hebrew, using William Romaine's edition of Calasio's concordance and lexicon. He was led to enquire into the famous preacher's evangelical doctrines, which in turn awakened in him concern for his spiritual state and ultimately to his conversion.

He became a firm and faithful advocate of 'justification by faith' and he soon abandoned the legal profession and prepared for the ministry in the Established Church of Ireland. He was ordained in 1792 and sought to express his evangelical beliefs whenever the opportunity afforded itself. He found common ground with Rev Rowland Hill (uncle of the postal reformer) who was preaching and lecturing in Ireland. The Archbishop of Dublin, Dr Fowler, opposed the evangelical school and sought to impose restrictions on Kelly and his supporters. Eventually the churches of Dublin were closed to him and this he found reprehensible. For a time Kelly preached in non-episcopal chapels in Dublin. In effect he was a dissenter and on principle took the path of separation. He established an independent denomination - congregational in form - and having sufficient financial resources was able to build places of worship at Athy, Portarlington, Wexford and Waterford. Incidentally, his wealth came from two sources - his late father's estate and from his wife's family, the Tighes of Wicklow.

He was possessed of an energetic personality and gathered considerable congregations to hear his powerful discourses. He was described as a "magnificent preacher and popular with the people." A man of varied learning, he knew several Oriental languages and was a notable Bible scholar. He lived out his beliefs and it is recorded that his generosity was particularly recognised during the days of the Famine of 1847. His liberality made him beloved of the poor as he gave of his substance while also proclaiming the "Bread of Life."

He ministered the Word for a remarkable sixty-three years, each year selflessly given to the Master's cause. His watchword was "Do all to the Glory of God." An old friend, Lord Plunkett, met him one day in later life, and said, "You will live to a great age, Mr Kelly!" "Yes," was Kelly's reply, "I am confident I shall - as I expect never to die!" His pulpit ministry ended in 1853 when he sustained a stroke from which he never recovered. He lingered for several months until his home-call at the age of eighty-four. His last words were, "Not my will, but thine."

As intimated above the Cross of Christ was a constant theme of Kelly's poetry, equally he embroidered praise to the Lord throughout his works. Consider the titles of his hymns: 'Hark 10,000 harps and voices', 'Who is this that comes from Edom', 'Behold the Lamb', 'Come ye saints', 'Praise the Saviour' and 'Lo, He cometh'.

The seventh edition of his hymns appeared in 1853 and contained 767 pieces. His preface includes the following remarks:

"It will be perceived that though there is an interval between the first edition and the last of nearly sixty years, both speak of the same great truths. In the course of that long period, the author has seen much and heard much; but nothing that he has seen or heard has made the least change in his mind as to the grand truths of the Gospel. What pacified the conscience then, does so now. What gave hope then, does so now. 'Other foundation can no man lay than that is laid, which is Jesus Christ'. "

Kelly was also the author of 'Andrew Dunn', a controversial narrative against Romanism and of a pamphlet entitled 'Thoughts on Imputed Righteousness'. Both publications had much merit but neither had the enduring quality of his sacred poems.

"Look, ye saints, the sight is glorious;
See the Man of sorrows now
From the fight returned victorious,
Every knee to Him shall bow;
Crown Him! Crown Him!
Crowns become the Victor's brow.

Hark, those bursts of acclamation!
Hark, those loud triumphant chords!
Jesus takes the highest station:
O what joy the sight affords!
Crown Him! Crown Him!
King of kings and Lord of lords!"

THOMAS KELLY 1769-1854

Chapter Ten

JAMES MONTGOMERY
POET, PRISONER AND PHILANTHROPIST

In the early nineteenth century there was opposition within the Church of England to the practice of using hymnbooks. John Wesley had used hymnbooks the previous century but any attempt to introduce a similar publication to the Anglican church provoked a strong reaction and threats of legal sanctions. When 'Cotterill's Selection' appeared, a court case loomed and those instrumental in its production faced ecclesiastical censure. This publication of evangelical hymns was withdrawn but Thomas Cotterill and his assistant James Montgomery, vowed to continue their work. They eventually succeeded with a new edition; each hymn had to be approved by Archbishop Vernon Harcourt.

James Montgomery was born at Irvine in Ayrshire, the son of a Moravian minister, an Ulster-Scot. For a short time the family lived in Gracehill, near Ballymena. Later they removed to Fulneck, in Yorkshire, where James attended a Moravian school. He received a good education but after his parents were sent as missionaries to the West Indies he concluded that he was unfit to fulfil the family's desire for him to be a minister, and ran away! After various adventures he settled in Sheffield, an assistant to a printer named

Gales. When Gales had to flee the country following the reaction to some political articles, James assumed the mantle and continued where his master left off. His material proved to be just as controversial and resulted in prosecution. He twice suffered fines and was imprisoned in York Castle!

Using the pseudonym "Gabriel Silvertongue," he wrote a series of articles in his unregenerate days against the Bible. When he was converted, some ten years later, he made strenuous efforts to seek out every copy of his essays in order to destroy them. Thereafter he employed his pen in writing poetry and some 400 hymns. On one occasion the question was put to him - "Which of your poems will live on?" He replied - "None, except a few of my hymns." True to his own words, his poetry is forgotten, but his sacred compositions survive. In his day his poetic genius was publicly acknowledged and he was awarded a government pension of £200 per annum.

John Ellerton, the author of 'The day Thou gavest', described Montgomery as the "first Englishman who collected and criticised hymns and who made people understand something of what a hymn meant and what it ought to be." Montgomery wrote that in all his hymns he had sought to reflect some human emotion, which had been his own experience, in the expectation that some soul would be profited thereby. Familiar to many will be the following hymns: 'Stand up and bless the Lord', 'Hail to the Lord's anointed', and 'For ever with the Lord'. Of all his compositions 'Hail to the Lord's anointed', is considered to be the finest rendering of Psalm 72, a Messianic Psalm. 'For ever with the Lord', which originally had twenty-two verses, remained unnoticed and unsung for twenty-five years until someone edited it and set it to music. It gained more indications of approval than any other of his works.

" 'For ever with the Lord!'
Amen, so let it be!
Life from the dead is in that word
'Tis immortality,
Here in the body pent,
Absent from Him I roam,
Yet nightly pitch my moving tent
A day's march nearer home."

Montgomery's service for the Lord was demonstrated in many directions throughout his long life. He was a keen worker on behalf of overseas missions, a supporter of the distribution of the Scriptures, an advocate for the abolition of slavery and a campaigner for social reform. He formed an association for the rescue of young boys employed to climb up industrial chimneys as sweeps - a cause later championed by Lord Shaftesbury. His interest in children's Sunday schools prompted him to write 'Prayer is the soul's sincere desire'. The hymn was titled 'What is prayer?' and was circulated in Nonconformist Sunday schools throughout Sheffield. The majestic theme was quickly appreciated beyond the intended sphere and it still is sung to great profit.

JAMES MONTGOMERY 1771-1854

"IT IS OF COURSE TRUE THAT HYMNS CANNOT BE SEPARATED FROM THEIR TUNES. THEY ARE WRITTEN TO BE SUNG, AND A GOOD HYMN REQUIRES A GOOD TUNE TO MAKE IT FULLY EFFECTIVE. BUT IN THE END THE WORDS MATTER MOST."

CANON FRANK COLQUHOUN

Chapter Eleven

REGINALD HEBER
MISSIONARY BISHOP TO INDIA

O ur subject came from an old and wealthy Yorkshire family, which could trace their lineage back to the 1400's. His father was both the Rector of Hodnet and the squire of Malpas, and so it came about that Reginald was brought up with a privileged lifestyle. He had an impressive academic career, graduating from Oxford with a B.A. and later M.A. degrees, and a list of prizes for poems and essays. Elevated by social position and his education, he yet had a humble nature with a genuine concern and compassion for the poor and the oppressed.

For years he stood almost alone - among his fellow students, the squires of England and the chaplains of the Anglican church - in his personal support for missionary and Bible societies and in co-operation with nonconformists. "He was for Christ and he loved and did much to elevate the Reformed church; he worked with all good men," said one admirer. Perhaps his evangelical views were reinforced by some of Hodnet's heritage: among many treasures, the church possessed a copy of Bishop Jewel's attack on the Roman Catholic Church!

In 1811 he began to produce hymns at a regular pace and by 1820 he had collected a sufficient number to warrant the publication of a missionary hymnbook, something which had not been issued before. He approached the Archbishop of Canterbury, Dr Manners Sutton, with a well argued proposal but permission was refused. Undeterred, Heber proceeded to have his hymns copied into note-books and these were circulated for congregational singing. His personal choice for music was a selection of Scottish airs rather than the traditional and monotonous tunes of the church. Incidentally, it was not until 1899 that the Anglican Missionary Hymnbook eventually appeared.

The absence of a suitable hymnbook with a missionary theme, was a dilemma for Dean Shipley when he was to preach on behalf of the "Society for the Propagation of the Gospel in Foreign Lands." Shipley asked his son-in-law Heber to provide an appropriate item for the climax of the service to be held in Wrexham Church on Whit Sunday, 1819. The request was made on the Saturday night before! Heber hastily wrote out a composition of four verses and entitled it 'From Greenland's icy mountains'. It was sung the next day and it has remained a classic ever since. The reference to Greenland was due to missionary endeavour there at the time and India and Ceylon appear because of Heber's personal interest in the needs of the sub-continent.

In 1822 Heber was offered the Bishopric of Calcutta. He initially refused but on the second request accepted. In this new office he exerted himself for three years with selfless devotion and energy to the physical and spiritual needs of the subcontinent. His diocese included not just the area around Calcutta, but also the whole of India and Ceylon. His hymn proved prophetic indeed!

"From Greenland's icy mountains,
From India's coral strand,
Where Africa's sunny fountains
Roll down their golden sand,
From many an ancient river,
From many a palmy plain,
They call us to deliver
Their land from error's chain."

Heber died suddenly after an exhausting and laborious day in the sweltering heat. The news of his demise was announced at the army garrison at Trichinopoly and immediate steps were taken for the burial of the second Lord Bishop of Calcutta, the Chief Missionary of the East, the sweet singer of the Church and a man greatly beloved. The funeral was an impressive one and full military honours were accorded to Heber. As his bishop's appointment was a Royal one, the British Government arranged for a memorial stone to be placed at his grave. The tablet commemorating his death reads: "Be ye also ready." There can't be many such government paid exhortations!

Heber's daughter Emily, married the grandson of Archbishop Sutton and other daughter Harriet Sarah was wed to the son of his greatest friend. His widow, some time later, married Count Valsamachi, a diplomat.

The legacy of Heber's pen extends to some 57 hymns plus a collection of literary reviews and classical poems. In current usage are his great missionary hymn mentioned above, and 'Holy, Holy, Holy, Lord God Almighty', 'The Son of God goes forth to war', and 'By cool Siloam's shady rill'. Heber has with justification been compared with William Cowper for his contribution to English hymnody.

In the 'Book of Praise', published in 1863 we find that of 412 hymns which satisfied Lord Selborne's criteria of a good hymn - "simplicity, freshness, and reality of feeling; a consistent elevation of tone, and a rhythm easy and harmonious"- eleven were by Cowper and fourteen by Heber. The esteem that Heber was held in, can be seen by the tributes paid by such figures as Alfred Lord Tennyson, who pronounced the hymn 'Holy, Holy, Holy,' as the finest in the English language.

"Holy, holy, holy, Lord God Almighty!
Early in the morning our song shall rise to Thee;
Holy, holy, holy, merciful and mighty,
God in three persons, blessed Trinity!"

W M Thackeray writing in 'The Four Georges' said of Heber:

"The charming poet, the happy possessor of all sorts of gifts and accomplishments ....beloved in his own home of Hodnet, counselling the people in their trouble, advising them in their difficulties, kneeling often at their sick beds at the hazard of his own life; where there was strife, the peacemaker; where there was want, the free giver."

REGINALD HEBER 1783-1826

"IN PRAYER WE ACT LIKE MEN; IN PRAISE WE ACT LIKE ANGELS."

THOMAS WATSON, PURITAN DIVINE

Chapter Twelve

HENRY FRANCIS LYTE
AUTHOR OF A NATIONAL HYMN

'The Times' newspaper recently reported the result of a poll on favourite hymns. Several thousand people gave their choice of three hymns in order of preference. A 'top ten' was thus produced and in fourth position was a hymn written by our present subject. The hymn was 'Abide with me', recognised as a National hymn, sung with feeling whether at Westminster Abbey or at Wembley Stadium!

H F Lyte was born in the village of Ednam, near Kelso in Scotland. His father, whom he probably never met, left his wife with three young boys to raise. He partially accepted his parental responsibilities by having his older sons placed in Portora Royal School, Enniskillen. The two boys were soon to be orphaned and only the charitable spirit of Dr Burrowes, the headmaster, in agreeing to act as foster father, rescued them from a Poor Law Institution. Lyte later refunded to his benefactor the whole cost of his education. From Portora Lyte entered Trinity College, Dublin. It was the original intention for him to pursue a career in medicine and accordingly his studies began. However these were abandoned and he switched to theology.

Following his graduation in 1814 he remained in Ireland and was soon appointed the curate of Taghmon, near Wexford. He removed to Cornwall two years later and in 1823 was appointed the perpetual curate of Lower Brixham in South Devon. Incidentally, it was in Cornwall that Lyte met the lady who became his wife. She was the daughter of a Methodist minister and she held to her own denominational views so strongly that her Anglican husband had to take her to her church each Sunday, while he travelled to his church alone!

His final curacy was to last twenty-four years in Brixham where his church overlooked the famous bay. From there the men of Devon had set sail to meet the Spanish Armada in 1588, and a hundred years later where William Prince of Orange landed to defend the Protestant Faith. Lyte was rightly proud of the rich heritage in that area. He had friendly ties with others of like faith but the presence of a new religious group tested him sorely. Quite a number of his congregation began to associate with the Plymouth Brethren and their departure took its toll upon his health.

It was the physical condition of another that had a profound effect and brought about a dramatic change in his life; this was when he was in Marazion, Cornwall. A brother minister who was seriously ill and close to death, appealed to him for spiritual life, which of course was not his to give. Finding no counsel within themselves, they resorted to study of the Bible. Both were led to see in Christ the only one who could deal with their soul's condition and give to them everlasting life. He wrote that he was brought to look at life and death "with a different eye than before; I began to study my Bible and preach in another manner than I had previously done."

Lyte thus spread the Word with a holy zeal that he had lacked and knew nothing about before. This was reflected in his preaching and in his poetry. His evangelistic passion led him to present a copy of the Bible to the crew of each ship which sailed from the busy fishing port. He also started a school for fishermen of all ages; in those days even young boys were sent to sea. When textbooks were not available to purchase, Lyte set to the task of writing suitable material.

He exerted the same energy with his Sunday school and Bible class, which numbered up to 800 scholars with over 70 teachers. His untiring efforts to witness to the whole town were demonstrated at holidays and fish-landings. He organised parades of children and fishermen to his church for special services, thus preventing them from squandering their hard earned wages on gambling and drink. His evangelistic address had a sobering effect as well!

Unfortunately Lyte's health declined - he had tuberculosis - and this dictated that before the onset of winter he would have to seek a milder climate. As September 1847 approached he was unable to preach but anticipated his departure to the Mediterranean. His daughter recorded that the family were surprised and almost alarmed when Lyte announced his intention of preaching once more to his people. "His weakness, and the possible danger attending the effort, were urged to prevent it, but in vain. It is better, as he used to say, to 'wear out than to rust out!' He did preach and amid the breathless attention of his hearers gave them a sermon on the Holy Communion."

He afterwards assisted in the administration of the Communion and felt much exhausted by the exertion, yet his friends had no reason to believe that it had been hurtful to him. That same evening (September 4th), perhaps with some sense that his life's work had come to a close, he handed his daughter a poem or rather a hymn with music of his own composing. The title was 'Abide with me', based on the words of Luke 24 v 29. In his memoirs, he noted that the hymn was written "when things were in a difficult state, when all around me seemed as I recalled it in a state of change and decay, and when one's own health was failing, it does greatly test one's faith in God."

Within a few days the family travelled to the South of France for the winter's recuperation but my mid-November Lyte's health had deteriorated. On the 20th of the month he passed away, his last words being "Peace - Joy!"

Over eighty hymns are attributed to Lyte and apart form 'Abide with me' and 'Praise my soul, the King of Heaven', perhaps only 'Jesus, I my cross have taken' attains a position of excellence. Each day the bells of All Saint's in Brixham, which was built as a memorial to Lyte, play 'When at Thy footstool Lord', 'Praise my soul, the King of Heaven' and 'Abide with me' at 8 a.m., noon, and 8 p.m. respectively.

> "Abide with me: fast falls the eventide;
> The darkness deepens; Lord with me abide!
> When other helpers fail, and comforts flee,
> Help of the helpless, O abide with me."
>
> I need Thy presence every passing hour;
> What but Thy grace can foil the tempter's power?
> Who like Thyself my guide and stay can be?
> Through cloud and sunshine, Lord abide with me."

HENRY FRANCIS LYTE 1793-1847

"THE VERY ACT OF PRAISE RELEASES THE POWER OF GOD INTO A SET OF CIRCUMSTANCES AND ENABLES GOD TO CHANGE THEM IF THIS BE HIS DECISION."

MERLIN R. CAROTHERS, NORTH AMERICAN CHAPLAIN

Chapter Thirteen

CHRISTOPHER WORDSWORTH
THE PROTESTANT BISHOP

The Wordsworth family has contributed much to the world of literature, but the name is also associated with the Established Church in which several generations have served. Christopher was the son and grandson of Anglican ministers, the nephew (and later the biographer) of the famous poet and the youngest of three brothers. They excelled in learning and each took away every academic award in their respective universities.

He had an extraordinarily brilliant education and became a Fellow and Classical Lecturer at Trinity College, Cambridge. In 1836 he was presented with the appointments of both Public Orator of his university and headmaster of Harrow. He held various charges before becoming minister in a Berkshire village. There he laboured for twenty-four years until he was elevated to occupy the Bishopric of Lincoln.

He was a diligent writer, publishing sermons and addresses, an eight volume commentary on the Bible (which gained the commendation of Dean Burgon), books on Greece and an anthology of hymns. He maintained a scholarly opposition to the

Church of Rome. His sermons of 1828 reveal his denunciations of Popery; these followed a visit to various Continental countries where he saw spiritual darkness at first hand. His evangelical crusade against Anglo-Catholicism in the church and rampant Popery in the nation was articulated in his controversial work "Union with Rome." He argued that the Roman system was the Harlot Church of Revelation 17. The propagandists for the Vatican were silenced and they failed to take up Wordsworth's challenge. Copies of his thesis were deliberately bought up just to remove it from circulation; however the book still remains a classic and is well worth a read.

When Pope Pius IX issued a papal letter in 1868, addressed to all "Protestants and non-Catholics," denouncing their separation from the "True Faith" and thereby excommunicating them, it was Wordsworth who replied in a learned pamphlet published in Latin and later translated into several languages. His response to the Pope was vigorous and pointed, suffice to quote:- "Dost thou suppose that thou hast excommunicated us by your words. No, rather thou hast excommunicated thyself. We, on our side have Christ; we have the Apostles; we have the Apostolic and Universal Church. Thou hast separated thyself from Christ."

It was when he took up the charge in Berkshire in 1844 that he wrote his enduring hymn 'O Lord of Heaven'. His parishioners had apparently never been taught that "it is more blessed to give than to receive." They were ready to accept parish handouts but proved reluctant to demonstrate their gratitude in a practical manner. He believed that the hymn would be more convincing than a sermon on charitable giving! The hymn is carefully constructed; at the commencement God is glorified and in the following verses he records the blessing of God's gifts in Creation, Christ, the Comforter and in character. How much praise and gratitude is due to the Lord who "hast made me glad through Thy works." He wrote that the first duty of a hymn-writer was to teach sound doctrine and thus to save souls.

Another of Wordsworth's hymns to be found in current hymnbooks, is 'O day of rest and gladness', one of the few compositions on the Lord's Day.

When illness overcame the Bishop and his departure from this mortal world was anticipated, he found great comfort in his favourite text of Scripture: "Rejoice in the Lord alway." The same text hung above his bed and was later to be inscribed at his grave. The affection with which he was held was expressed in many ways at his funeral. Local schoolchildren came to his home and sang the hymn 'Brief life is here our portion', many dignitaries attended the Cathedral service and even the Lincoln horse races were postponed as a mark of respect. Alas none of his successors have emulated the Protestant stand of Christopher Wordsworth.

"O Lord of heaven, and earth, and sea,
To Thee all praise and glory be;
How shall we show our love to Thee,
Who gavest all?"

CHRISTOPHER WORDSWORTH 1807-1885

"THE MAKERS OF GOOD BALLADS ARE SAID TO SWAY NATIONAL OPINION. THE WRITERS OF GOOD HYMNS, IN LIKE MANNER, ARE THOSE WHO LEAVE THE DEEPEST MARKS ON THE FACE OF THE CHURCH."

J C RYLE

Chapter Fourteen

ANDREW YOUNG
SCHOOLMASTER AND POET

The beautiful and historic City of Edinburgh has been the birth place of many great men of literature. The name of Andrew Young is not one which comes to mind as being in that category, but in his lifetime he was recognised as one of Scotland's noted poets. The capitol city was the place of his early education and university training which was to equip him for a career in teaching. He spent eight years altogether in literary and theological instruction and this led to early promotion to be headmaster of Niddry Street school. Later he was appointed to principalship of a college at St. Andrews University.

He retired while in his forties and returned to his native city to devote his time to worthwhile causes and to maintain association with various scientific and educational institutions. That is not to say that he lived in an 'ivory tower', aloof from the harsh conditions and uncertainties of mid-Victorian life. He was very much in touch with reality as he was involved in his church, Greenside Parish. There he was elected elder and acted as superintendent of the Sunday School, encountering two and three generations of some families during his thirty years in the post.

Young is remembered for his children's hymn 'There is a happy land'. Surely no other hymn for the young has been such a universal favourite. As to its origin he wrote that he had been spending a social evening with a company of friends, one of whom was playing various pieces at the piano. Among these was a "sweet and tender air, which charmed me exceedingly. On asking the name of it, I was told that it was an Indian tune called 'Happy Land'." It immediately occurred to him that such a melody could not fail to be popular if wedded to appropriate words.

The words 'Happy Land' began a chain of thought which culminated in the composition we now know. Many stories have been attached to the hymn since its publication in 1838. Perhaps the most touching concerns the novelist W M Thackeray. The author of 'Vanity Fair' was travelling through a London slum and he heard street children - "of a most ragged appearance"- singing 'There is a happy land'. The contrast between their squalor and the splendour of the subject of the song, struck him so forcibly that he was moved to tears.

The 'Happy Land' is of course Heaven, happy for there is no darkness nor dying, no pain nor crying, no sin nor sighing. Happy too by far, for the Lord God Almighty and the Saviour dwell therein.

A few days before Young journeyed to that Happy Land he was thrilled to read Dr John G Paton's book of his missionary labours. There was a reference to the fact that a native chief had been converted through the words of the children's hymn. Young thereupon wrote in his journal "Glory to God in the Highest!"

"There is a happy land
Far, far away,
Where saints in glory stand,
Bright, bright as day.
O how they sweetly sing:
Worthy is our Saviour King!
Loud let His praises ring,
Praise, praise for aye.

Bright in that happy land,
Beams every eye;
Kept by a Father's hand,
Love cannot die;
On then to glory run;
Be a crown and kingdom won;
And, bright above the sun,
Reign reign for aye."

ANDREW YOUNG 1807-1889

"HYMNS CHEER WITH HEAVENLY MESSAGES THE HARD BURDENS OF LIFE; THEY HAVE BEEN THE WORDS OF THANKSGIVING ON THE LIPS OF A LIBERATED SOUL; THEY HAVE GIVEN COURAGE TO THE SUFFERING; THEY HAVE BORNE THE NAME OF JESUS FAR AND WIDE, AND HAVE HELPED TO WRITE IT DEEP ON COUNTLESS SOULS."

ANONYMOUS

Chapter Fifteen

JOHN SAMUEL BEWLEY MONSELL

WHO FOUGHT THE GOOD FIGHT

Writing in 1862, Dr Monsell criticised Victorian singing of hymns in church. He stated, "we are too distant and reserved in our praises. We sing not as if our hearts were on fire with the flame of divine love and joy, as we should sing to Him and of Him, Who is chief among ten thousand and 'altogether lovely'. If we loved him as we ought, we would not be so cold." Such remarks would have been considered revolutionary had they been articulated by anyone else, but Monsell, one-time chaplain to Bishop Mant and respected pastor, had gained a reputation as a poet and hymnwriter of no mean talent.

He gave the church an overall collection of three hundred hymns, of which seventy-two are deemed "best known." Seven hymns were to appear in the Irish Church Hymnal, a testimony in itself to the quality of Monsell's compositions. His precept to encourage worthy praise was fulfilled in such hymns as 'O worship the King in the beauty of Holiness' , 'Christ is risen, Hallelujah!' and 'Fight the good fight with all thy might'.

Monsell was born in Londonderry when his father was curate in Limavady (but was soon to be appointed Archdeacon of the historic St Columbs Cathedral). Following his graduation at Trinity College Dublin, Monsell was ordained as curate in the Maiden City in 1834. The history of the city of his birth with its record of battles and seige impressed him, and the relics of the Seige displayed in the Cathedral fascinated him from an early age. 'Fight the good fight' was written with the backdrop of the City and the lessons of Scripture before him. He began to write poetry and prose as a young curate and maintained the art for forty years, publishing several small volumes of his works. His hymns were described by Dr John Julian as "bright and joyous and musical - though only a few are of enduring excellence." Many will disagree and more than one writer has commented that Monsell's talent has still not been fully appreciated.

Each verse of 'Fight the good fight' alludes to the four characters in Paul's second letter to Timothy (4 v 7-8): the soldier fighting, the athlete running, the pilgrim trusting and the believer bearing. It is essentially spiritual and yet distinctly personal as it deals with the Christian's daily life.

"Fight the good fight with all thy might;
Christ is thy strength, and Christ thy right;
Lay hold on life, and it shall be
Thy joy and crown eternally.

Run the straight race through God's good grace,
Lift up thine eyes, and seek his face;
Life with its path before thee lies,
Christ is the way, and Christ the prize."

After Londonderry, Monsell ministered in three other Ulster churches: St Mary Magdalene (Donegall Pass, Belfast), Dunaghy (Clough) and Ramoan (Ballycastle). Thereafter he removed to England, eventually becoming rector of St Nicholas' in Guildford. He was no idle dreamer and where work was to was needed, he was not found wanting. Both at Ramoan and Guildford he launched into the rebuilding of neglected church property. Sadly it was when he was inspecting progress of the reconstruction of the roof of St Nicholas' that he was to meet with a tragic accident. Falling masonry struck him and he sustained injuries from which he did not recover.

His last literary effort had been to compose a few lines to raise funds for the renovation. He entitled the piece 'Near Home, at last!' The opening verse was prophetic:

"Dear body, thou and I must part,
Thy busy hand, thy throbbing heart
Must cease to work and cease to play
For me at no far distant day."

J S B MONSELL 1811-1875

"THE MOST ENDURING HYMNS ARE BORN IN THE SILENCES OF THE SOUL, AND NOTHING MUST BE ALLOWED TO INTRUDE WHILE THEY ARE BEING FRAMED INTO LANGUAGE."

FANNY J CROSBY

Chapter Sixteen

THOMAS HORNBLOWER GILL
A PATRIOTIC POET

I t should be understood that many hymns as we now have them, are not as they were originally written. Every generation has taken liberties with the sacred poems of others. There have been some notable improvements and there have been those distorted to please the melody writer!

Over the years one hymn written by Gill has been subjected to repeated alteration: 'Lord in the fullness of my might', which was written in 1855 and entitled 'Early Love'. By 1874 the published version appears without the original first verse but begins with what was the final verse! The lost opening lines began "With sin, I would not make abode." Gill was not ungrateful for the changes to his work and commented that some of his hymns had been improved and strengthened by the modifications. Truly the present version has much to commend it.

Gill was born in Birmingham of parents who belonged to Presbyterian families of Puritan stock, but had become Unitarian in doctrine and religious practice. This background was to deny him entrance to Oxford University in 1838. A necessary test for admission was subscription to the Thirty-Nine Articles of Faith, but his hereditary Unitarianism forbade him. So he commenced his studies of historical and theological subjects in isolation.

He discovered the Puritan theology that his family had abandoned and he delighted in the history of the Reformation and Non-Conformity. He began to read the Greek New Testament and he rejoiced that it "clearly showed me that Unitarianism failed to interpret the Book of Life. As truth after truth broke upon my gaze, God put a new song into my mouth." He thus forsook heresy and embraced the Truth.

He was greatly impressed by the poetry of Isaac Watts, and it is no doubt to his influence that Gill's hymns have a message and such a depth of meaning. He was to compose about 200 pieces, of which 80 were used in public worship. Dr John Julian, the hymnologist, says that Gill belongs to a small company of really original hymnists and he describes his hymns as being distinguished with "keen discernment of the Spirit of the Gospel, with profound thought and Scriptural themes." His sacred pieces were to be found almost exclusively in Baptist and Congregational collections but gradually they were accepted among other denominations.

Gill was an unashamed patriot and Protestant; he bypassed the Unitarian phase in his family history and relished his descent "from a Moravian martyr and an ejected minister. I rejoice not a little in the godly Protestant stock from which I spring." His hero was Oliver Cromwell. His hymn beginning "Lord dost Thou never Thy servants bless" is based on the words of the Protector, and below the title of 'Early Love' he quoted Cromwell's comment - "How good it is to close with Christ."

His writings include 'The Anniversaries', (a poem commemorating great men and events in Protestant history), 'The Papal Drama', (a trenchant assault on Romanism) and 'Luther's Birthday', a further collection of historical poems. He described his hymn 'O'er fullness of Grace, blest Britain rejoice', as the thanksgiving song of Protestant Britain.

"Lord in the fulness of my might
I would for Thee be strong;
While runneth o'er each dear delight,
To Thee should soar my song.

O choose me in my golden time,
In my dear joys have part!
For Thee the glory of my prime,
The fulness of my heart!"

THOMAS HORNBLOWER GILL 1819-1906

"THERE IS NO PRINCIPAL ELEMENT OF CHRISTIANITY; THERE IS NO MORAL OR ETHICAL SENTIMENT PECULIARLY CHARACTERISTIC OF THE GOSPEL; NO HEIGHT OR DEPTH OF FEELING PROPER TO THE SPIRITUAL LIFE, THAT DOES NOT FIND ITSELF CLEARLY CONVEYED IN MANY OF OUR WELL-KNOWN HYMNS."

ISAAC TAYLOR, DISSENTING PREACHER

Chapter Seventeen

JosepH MedicotT ScriveN
WHOSE HYMN IS WISE COUNSEL

Joseph Scriven is well known as the writer of the famous hymn 'What a Friend we have in Jesus'. There are various reminders in his home town of Banbridge which perpetuate his memory: there is the impressive monument adjacent to the local Council offices and on a secluded road approaching the outskirts of the town is the home of his birth. His hymn has encircled the globe and is beloved by countless believers. It was a hymn written from the heart, out of the real experience of adversity and sorrow. Its lines are expressions of wise counsel, to be heeded in the fluctuating circumstances of life. Scriven spoke of the things that he knew and of the answer that he found.

He was born in 1819 in Ballymoney Lodge, about a mile outside Banbridge - the house can be seen from the main Newry Road. His father was a military man, a captain in the Royal Marines. At the age of fifteen Joseph was sent off to Trinity College in Dublin, but after two years his father encouraged him to enrol at Addiscomb Military College in Surrey. The intention was that he would become an officer cadet and would be attached to the East India

Company. Joseph was unable to complete the course due to ill-health and returned to Banbridge to live at Seapatrick. He decided to return to his studies at Trinity and he completed his BA degree at the age of 23.

The family were members of the Church of Ireland but the son of the house showed no religious convictions and had no particular desire to enter the ministry. He led an aimless existence until romance lifted his spirits! This relationship with a local girl blossomed to proposed matrimony and the couple prepared for their future life together. It was on the eve of their marriage that tragedy struck. His betrothed was crossing the River Bann when her horse threw her and she drowned in full view of her lover, who watched helplessly from the opposite bank. The loss was devastating and it seemed that Scriven was beyond consoling.

The tragedy directed him to find comfort in the Lord, and more than that to find salvation from his sins. He became a member of the Brethren and this may have caused some friction in the family as he soon resolved to leave his native land and sail for Canada to begin life afresh. At first he settled at Rice Lake and afterwards at Port Hope, Ontario. He became a tutor to some families in the area and he also engaged in evangelism.

When times were hard he was not averse to doing physical work; in better times he secured employment in a dairy. Though a man of refinement, he chose a simple mode of life and had few possessions. His health was indifferent and this was probably self-inflicted as he would labour in the worst of conditions to provide for the poor and would give the clothes off his back to the needy. He was a man who was much respected for his acts of charity and his sacrificial attitude.

He became engaged to Miss Eliza Roche, a member of the Brethren and once again he looked forward to a happy future. Alas, this was not to be and their planned wedding in 1854 was repeatedly postponed as his intended failed to recover from pneumonia. She lingered for almost three years and her death was another bitter blow. Scriven slipped into a state of depression until again he found consolation in the Lord.

It was at his time - 1857 - that he penned his immortal hymn, which he called 'Pray without ceasing'. He maintained that the composition was not his but "the Lord and I did it between us." Each verse has its theme - sins, sorrows and sighs - all can be taken to the Lord in prayer. Originally the hymn was a personal and intimate message for himself but he decided to publish it along with a collection of other poems in 1869. The book was simply called 'Hymns and other verses'. In the providence of God, Charles Converse, an amateur musician who was also a lawyer and an inventor, read the hymn and decided to put music to it; this was in 1870.

Converse called his tune 'What a Friend we have in Jesus', being the first line of the hymn, and the two have been inextricably linked ever since. Ira Sankey wrote of the piece that "thousands have been cheered in time of trouble and so led nearer to Christ, by this sweet and simple hymn." Sankey became aware of the hymn in 1875 and at the last minute inserted it in one of his compilations. "Thus the last hymn that went into the book, became one of the first in favour"- he wrote in his biography.

Scriven's testimony was that 'he helped others' and his memorials record his benevolence and caring nature. Sadly his last days on earth were spent in poverty and sickness; more than one source details his death by drowning in 1886.

Perhaps no other hymn has had such a profound impact than 'What a Friend'.

"What a Friend we have in Jesus,
All our sins and griefs to bear!
What a privilege to carry
Everything to God in prayer!
O what peace we often forfeit,
O what needless pain we bear,
All because we do not carry
Everything to God in prayer.

Have we trials and temptations?
Is there trouble anywhere?

We should never be discouraged:
Take it to the Lord in prayer.
Can we find a friend so faithful,
Who will all our sorrows share?
Jesus knows our every weakness:
Take it to the Lord in prayer.

Are we weak and heavy-laden,
Cumbered with a load of care?
Precious Saviour, still our refuge:
Take it to the Lord in prayer,
Do thy friends despise, forsake thee?
Take it to the Lord in prayer;
In His arms He'll take and shield thee,
Thou wilt find a solace there."

JOSEPH MEDDICOT SCRIVEN 1819-1886.

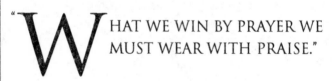

"WHAT WE WIN BY PRAYER WE
MUST WEAR WITH PRAISE."

MATTHEW HENRY, EXPOSITOR & MINISTER

Chapter Eighteen

GEORGE FREDERICK ROOT
COMPOSER FOR ALL OCCASIONS

Our present subject is probably responsible for writing and publishing more secular and sacred tunes than any other composer. Some of the pieces that he handled are well known to us, but more on that later!

At the age of thirteen, George Root was said to have been able to play a tune on as many instruments as his years. Music seemed to flow in his veins. He was brought up on a farm near Sheffield, Massachusetts, and it was apparent to all concerned that he was not destined to be a farmer! He was dispatched to Boston where his talent could be suitably cultivated! His rare ability and prowess on several instruments drew the attention of Dr Lowell Mason, the composer of the music of 'My faith looks up to Thee'. Mason hired him in 1840 to be an assistant for children's singing classes. He soon gained a reputation for his teaching skill. He also attracted popular attention through the secular pieces he was now composing.

In 1845 he achieved a post as music instructor at the New York Institution for the Blind, where he met another teacher, a former pupil of the school, a Miss Fanny Crosby. During the next five years the pair were to produce about 60 songs of a popular sentimental type until Miss Crosby forsook this activity to concentrate upon hymn-writing and other labours. Meanwhile Root travelled to Paris to direct his attention to studying singing and piano. He returned sufficiently well equipped to open an Institute for training teachers in various music disciplines. He began another new field of labour on Sundays, when he took his place at the organ of Mercer Street Presbyterian Church, New York.

His brother, Ebenezer Towner Root, was equally competent in music but preferred the publishing and commercial aspect. He partnered C M Cady to form 'Root & Cady' in 1858. It was two years later that George agreed to join the partnership and became chief of publication. He was a voluminous writer and was acknowledged as America's foremost composer of military songs, which gained widespread use during the Civil War. The publishing house circulated the 'Battle Cry of Freedom', 'Marching through Georgia' and 'Tramp, tramp, tramp'. These and many other tunes were adapted by several nations, and indeed some survive as marching tunes in our own province!

His diverse musical career was honoured by the profession in 1873 when he was presented with the degree of Doctor of Music at Chicago University. By this time, although still heavily committed to the 'Root & Cady' business, he was also producing musical pieces for Sunday Schools. His tune 'Tramp, tramp, tramp' was better employed to accompany 'Jesus loves the little children'. 'When He cometh' and 'Ring the bells of Heaven' were sung to his tunes. He supplied both the words and music of 'Come to the Saviour' and 'Why do wait dear brother?'

Dr Root was a man of singularly gracious and engaging personality; a man who delighted in music, was passionate about his convictions and was sincere about his religious principles. He set as his aim in his martial, patriotic and sacred compositions, some motivation or thought to aspire to high ideals. He died on August 6, 1895 and his request was honoured that nothing be sung at his funeral but the Doxology by Ken. He left a wonderful legacy of great and stirring tunes and of course many hymns.

GEORGE FREDERICK ROOT

Surely his supreme composition was 'She only touched the hem of His garment'. Based on the account found in Matthew 9 verse 20, the hymn has well been described as a "miracle pen picture."

"She only touched the hem of His garment
As to His side she stole,
Amid the crowd that gathered around Him,
And straightway she was whole.

O touch the hem of His garment
And thou, too, shalt be free;
His saving power - this very hour
Shall give new life to thee."

GEORGE FREDERICK ROOT 1820-1895

"PEOPLE STILL PREFER THE OLDER HYMNS BECAUSE THE WORDS ARE GOOD POETRY AND GOOD THEOLOGY - THAT STRIKES A NOTE IN THEIR HEARTS."

HARRY BRAMMA, DIRECTOR OF THE ROYAL SCHOOL OF CHURCH MUSIC

Chapter Nineteen

WILLIAM ORCUTT CUSHING
EVANGELIST AND HYMNWRITER

Wiliam Cushing was born on the last day of 1823 in Hingham, Massachusetts, into a family where God was worshipped and His word cherished. From his earliest days William became familiar with the Gospel and when still in his youth, in simple childlike faith he put his trust in the Lord Jesus Christ. He bore a consistent testimony, and kept in his heart a belief that the Lord had some special service for him to perform. He was keen to do whatever he could in the Lord's work and when he heard the call to enter the ministry he sincerely felt that this was the fulfilment of his secret longing.

He became an active and enthusiastic evangelist in his own town and along the east coast of the USA. After many years of faithful preaching, his ministry took a new and unexpected direction. He suffered an affliction which must be the fear of every public speaker, and that was to his voice. One can but imagine the frustration for a preacher to lose the very faculty upon which their objective depends.

He experienced deep disappointment at not being able to proclaim the Gospel, but the Lord showed him that he could yet speak and that was through the printed word. Better still his hymn-writing could be enjoyed by those who were blessed with a voice to sing. So Cushing embarked on a career, an unwelcome one at first, which was to prove more enduring than the spoken word.

He left a rich collection of hymns on various themes and for our benefit he detailed the circumstances of some of the compositions. 'Down in the valley with my Saviour I would go', with the familiar chorus 'Follow, follow, I would follow Jesus' was written out of a longing to give up all for Christ. This piece reflected much of the enthusiasm of his youth and went forth with the prayer and hope that some heart might be led to follow the Lord.

'Hiding in Thee' (Oh, safe to the Rock) was the result of "many tears, many heart conflicts and soul yearnings, of which the world can know nothing." We do not know indeed the spiritual battles that the writer endured, but what comfort is to be found in the words:

"How oft in the conflict, when pressed by the foe,
I have fled to my Refuge and breathed out my woe;
How often when trials like sea-billows roll,
Have I hidden in Thee, O Thou Rock of my soul."

Cushing had asked the Lord specifically that He would give him something that would glorify Him and at the same time be profitable to someone who might find solace in the Rock of his Salvation. That prayer was abundantly answered in that hymn.

Perhaps the most extraordinary circumstances surround the piece 'Beautiful valley of Eden'. One day, sometime in 1875, Cushing was communing with the Lord intent upon His blessing when suddenly there came upon his heart a vision of the heavenly country. "I seemed to look down upon a river that like a mighty tide rolled beneath me. I saw an enchanted land; its hills and valleys were sleeping in a heavenly calm. It was more beautiful than words can tell, and my heart seemed to be there." The vision remained until he had penned the hymn and only then did it gradually fade from his view. Some years later Cushing's words were enhanced by William Sherwin's melody.

Other compositions from his pen include 'There'll be no dark valley' (on the theme of the Second Coming of the Lord), 'Under His wings' (security and protection in the Lord), 'Ring the bells of Heaven' (peace and joy in salvation) and 'When He cometh'. The last mentioned is a delightful and beautiful children's hymn though enjoyed by those of all ages.

"When He Cometh, when He cometh
To make up His jewels,
All His jewels, precious jewels,
His loved and His own."

WILLIAM ORCUTT CUSHING 1823-1903

"THE CHURCH HAS A GREAT HERITAGE OF LITERATURE IN WHICH HYMNOLOGY OCCUPIES AN IMPORTANT PART. MEN AND WOMEN OF ALL NATIONS - HAVE IN THEIR HYMNS GIVEN BEAUTIFUL AND ENDURING EXPRESSION TO THEIR LOVE FOR THE LORD JESUS CHRIST."

JAMES DINWOODIE, CHILDREN'S EVANGELIST

Chapter Twenty

ELIZABETH CLEPHANE
& ANNE ROSS COUSIN
THE MELROSE DUET

The historic Scottish Border town of Melrose, immortalised by Sir Walter Scott in story and song, was the home of two lady writers Anne Cousin and Elizabeth Clephane. For a period of ten years the pair were friends and worshippers in the little Free Church, later known as St.Aidan's, but now demolished. The older lady was the wife of the minister and the younger a church member and benefactor. Each made an enduring contribution to the church universal with their inspiring poetry.

Miss Clephane had no literary aspirations and the popularity of her verse came many years after her death. By contrast Mrs Cousin was a well-known writer and her works were published and widely circulated in her lifetime. Different circumstances were to bring them to Melrose and to the same place of worship.

Elizabeth Cecilia Douglas Clephane was born in Edinburgh, where her father had his official residence as Sheriff of Fife. There were eventually six children in the family, three boys and three girls. They were proud of their ancestry, especially from their mother's side - she was a Douglas, an old Scottish family. (One of the twentieth century descendants became Conservative Prime Minister, Sir Alex Douglas-Home). When Sheriff Douglas died in 1838 the family moved to Ormiston but when their mother passed away, they removed to Melrose to be near to relatives. The double bereavement had a profound affect upon Elizabeth, who was described as "a very quiet child, shrinking from notice and always absorbed in books."

Further sorrow came to the home when the eldest son George was packed off to Canada as a "remittance man." This was a Victorian practice whereby a member of the family, sometimes a law-breaker, was paid an allowance to seek a new life in the Colonies.

In May 1851 George died following a fall in a drunken stupor on a lonely road in Fergus, Ontario. A much-weathered headstone in the graveyard of St Andrew's Church in Fergus records his passing away at the age of 32.

The three sisters bore the ill-tidings with fortitude; Elizabeth in particular harboured the belief that the lost sheep of a brother "had found pardon and peace through the Cross" before passing into Eternity.

Whether she committed her thoughts to paper at this time or many years later, it was not until 1868, that her poem 'The Lost Sheep' was printed in 'The Children's Hour' magazine, which was then edited by her cousin. In all she had eight pieces published, of which only two are now known. 'The Lost Sheep' is recognised today by the title 'There were Ninety and Nine'.

"There were ninety and nine that safely lay
In the shelter of the fold;
But one was out on the hills away,
Far off from the gates of gold,
Away on the mountains wild and bare,
Away from the tender Shepherd's care."

It was surely in the Providence of God that Ira Sankey read and kept a newspaper cutting containing a reprint of 'The Lost Sheep' and that he was led to compose the tune for it in such a unique way.

(See the story on Sankey). We can but speculate how many lost sheep have come to the Great Shepherd through Miss Clephane's hymn.

The other extant piece is 'Beneath the Cross of Jesus':

"Beneath the Cross of Jesus
I fain would take my stand,
The shadow of a mighty rock
Within a weary land;
A home within the wilderness
A rest upon the way,
From the burning of the noon-tide heat,
And the burden of the day."

In their latter years, the Clephane sisters exercised a quiet ministry of charity and compassion. There is a record of them selling their carriage and horses so that others could benefit financially from the proceeds. This meant for them a walk of several miles from their home at Bridgend House to and from the town of Melrose for all their shopping and social calls. Their generosity also ensured that their church did not have any debt.

Throughout her life Elizabeth Clephane was of delicate disposition but her death came quite unexpectedly. A beautiful tribute was made in 'A Remembrance of E. C. C. - 1830-1869' -

"We knew not that our life's delight
Was gliding from us day by day;
That unseen wings with silent flight,
Were bearing our beloved away.

While earthly shadows dimmed our eye
She saw the Bridegroom - heard His call;
And lifted her pure lamp on high
Walked with white feet into His hall."

The writer of this tribute was Anne Ross Cousin. She was born in 1824, the only daughter of Dr David Ross Cundell, who had served as a surgeon in the British navy and who was present at the Battle of Waterloo. Following her father's death, she lived in Edinburgh where she remained till her marriage to Rev William Cousin in 1847. At that time he was the minister of Chelsea Presbyterian Church but he was soon to accept a call to the Free Church at Irvine, Scotland. It was there that she wrote her great hymn 'The Sands of Time are sinking', which was first published in the "Christian Treasury"of 1857.

As one of the songs on Heaven it takes a deservedly high place in hymnody. Perhaps no other sacred piece on this theme, emphasises - as the secret of Heaven's attraction for the Christian heart - the personal presence of the Lamb that was slain. The hymn as we now have it is in fact a selection from her nineteen verse composition, the product of a long and loving study of the life and letters of Samuel Rutherford and founded on the dying words of the Scottish martyr: "Glory dwelleth in Immanuel's Land."

"The sands of time are sinking;
The dawn of Heaven breaks;
The summer morn I've sighed for,
The fair, sweet morn awakes.
Dark, dark hath been the midnight,
But day-spring is at hand,
And glory, glory dwelleth
In Immanuel's land."

Her book of devotional verse, compiled in 1876, also bore the same title. It was from this date that her hymn began to find acceptance and was to be included in the hymnals of the Scottish and English Presbyterian Churches.

The tune, which is so closely associated with it, is called 'Rutherford', and originated in the French Protestant church in the early 1800's and was anonymously altered to marry with the words.

Another of her hymns 'O Christ what burdens bowed Thy head' earned the appreciation of Ira Sankey. He wrote that the piece was invaluable in his mission services - "a hymn very much blessed." Dr John G Paton, the missionary to the New Hebrides, wrote a letter of personal thanks to the authoress and he recounted that her hymns had made a profound impression upon him, especially when he heard them sung by a large congregation. It was a source of quiet satisfaction for this lady writer that her humble poems gained such universal agreement.

No doubt her hymns were sung with much feeling in the little Free Church in Melrose, to where her husband had been called as minister in 1859. For twenty four years they served the Master in the Border town, the Rev Cousin with his preaching and Mrs Cousin with her sacred writing. She survived her husband by twenty-three years, spending these years in Edinburgh. "The dawn of Heaven" broke for her on December 6th 1906.

"PREACHING AND PRAYING SHALL ONE DAY CEASE FOREVER; BUT PRAISE SHALL NEVER DIE. PRAISE TRAINS MEN FOR HEAVEN, WHERE IT IS ONE OF THE PRINCIPAL OCCUPATIONS."

J C RYLE

Chapter Twenty One

ALBERT MIDLANE
WHO GAVE US CLASSIC HYMNS

Midlane was born in Newport, Isle of Wight, a short time after the sudden death of his father. Denied the blessings of a father's companionship and guidance, he enjoyed the compensating benefit of the counsel of a godly mother. He remembered his mother saying "They told me when your dear father died that my child would be the Lord's gift to cheer and help me in my widowhood."

She ensured that he was taught the way of the Lord at home and when he grew up she sought out a suitable Sunday School where sound instruction would advance his spiritual growth. She chose well, for his Sunday School teacher was a faithful instructor who left a lasting impression upon him. In later years he ascribed his successful efforts in writing sacred poetry to that teacher.

While still in his teenage years he enjoyed some popularity with his first hymn, which could be sung to a very recognisable tune - the National Anthem! It was called 'God bless our Sunday School'! He was to continue writing throughout his life and produced over 1000 items, of which about a third could be classified as hymns. Of that proportion only a handful take any significant place in modern hymnals.

'There's a Friend for little children' came to be written after Midlane had been meditating on the theme throughout the day, while he engaged in the routine duties of his hardware shop. After his family retired for the night, he remained at the fireside to contemplate further. Before sleep overcame him he had written six verses with the theme as its title. The original first line read "There's a rest for little children" and he later substituted "Friend."

The verses were scribbled in his note-book and for some months he kept them to himself. The hymn was published in December 1859 in a children's magazine, edited by C H Mackintosh. His identity was not disclosed beyond the initials "A M" but so much interest was generated that the name of the humble shopkeeper was eventually revealed. The announcement also ended speculation that others were responsible for the composition.

In Revival Year (1859) he produced 'Revive Thy work, O Lord' and later 'Passing onward, quickly passing' and 'Ever to the Saviour cling'. A contemporary, Josiah Miller, said of Midlane's hymns that they were "full of Scriptural thought, careful in their wording, and often very pleasing without reaching the highest form of poetical excellence." A marked feature of his pieces is the constant and happy use of Scriptural phrases.

Midlane stated that most of his hymns had been written "during walks around the historic ruins of Carisbrooke Castle. The twilight hour, so dear to thought, and the hushed serenity then pervading nature, have often allured my soul to deep and uninterrupted meditation." He also said that the absence of such walks probably denied the writing of some lines.

On one occasion the financial circumstances of the Midlane family came to be known and a public collection was taken up to relieve their plight; this proved to be a sad experience for one who was so rich in his spiritual life and who freely gave of his labour for the benefit of the Church worldwide.

At the beginning of 1909, there was a special service in London in St Paul's Cathedral to celebrate the fiftieth anniversary of Midlane's great hymn. The author was present as the honoured guest.

A choir of 3000 children sang his famous hymn to the tune 'In Memoriam', written by Sir John Stainer in 1875, commemorating the composer's son Frederick who "Jesus had called to Himself" the previous year.

In just a few weeks after the event Midlane was to take up residence in that home -

"Above the bright blue sky,
Where Jesus reigns in Glory,
A home of peace and joy.
No home on earth is like it,
Or can with it compare;
For every one is happy,
Nor could be happier, there."

ALBERT MIDLANE 1825-1909

"**H**YMNOLOGY IS A HAND-MAID TO MEDITATION AND AN INSPIRATION TO CONSECRATED EVANGELISM."

M GUTHRIE CLARK, WRITER

Chapter Twenty Two

AMELIA MATILDA HULL
WHOSE TESTIMONY SAVED HER FAMILY

I tinerant evangelists have travelled through the towns and villages of Britain for centuries. Many saw the results of their labours while others sowed the seed for another preacher's hire. One evangelist, in the mid- 1800's, held a tent mission in Exmouth, near to the cathedral city of Exeter. We know his text (John 3 verses 14-15) and we know the result of the sermon delivered, but we know not the preacher's name. The fruit from that faithful witness was Amelia Hull.

In God's mercy Amelia was brought to realise that the Lord Jesus Christ had died on Calvary for her sins, and that she could know forgiveness and could have assurance of salvation. The joy of her salvation was soon to be challenged. When she testified to her father, he denounced her for indulging in "religious madness" as he described it. He threatened physical violence if she persisted in her talk of having "sins forgiven." He was a retired army officer and local magistrate, and was well used to dispensing punishment.

Such a rebuke accompanied with the threats, drove her to the Scriptures, which were now read with an earnest desire for consolation. Therein she did find comfort and confidence. One verse was special to her:- "Look unto me and be ye saved," Isaiah 45 v 22. This was the same verse which C H Spurgeon also treasured. Meditating upon those words, she wrote the poem: 'There is life for a look at the Crucified One'. When the opportunity afforded itself, she presented the completed verses to her father, not quite certain as to how he would react but with the prayer that the Lord would do a work in his hardened heart. There was an outburst - but of tears, because he broke down, a humbled man, overcome with conviction of sin.

> "There is life for a look at the Crucified One,
> There is life at this moment for thee,
> Then look, sinner, look unto Him and be saved,
> Unto Him who was nailed to the tree.

> *Look, look, look and live;*
> *There is life for a look at the Crucified One,*
> *There is life at this moment for thee.*

He too cried unto the Lord for salvation and truly for him there was life "this moment for thee!" Amelia's testimony was thus honoured and opposition removed at the same time. The Hull household would never be the same again. The son of the family, Captain T H Hull, was serving in the Indian Army and he was written to about the "Good News" at home. Wonderfully, he came to Christ as well. He later returned home and settled in Exmouth, where the family became a noted force as they witnessed for Christ. They associated themselves with the Brethren and Capt. Hull proved himself to be a gifted preacher. The original Gospel Hall in the town was financed and built by the Hulls.

Amelia Hull lived a life of devotion and selfless service in the cause of Christ. While the family name has perished in the area in which they lived, Amelia's at least will be perpetuated as long as her poem, now hymn, 'Crucified One' is sung. The only other hymn to survive is 'I have been at the altar and witnessed the Lamb'.

"I have been at the altar and witnessed the Lamb
Burnt wholly to ashes for me;
And watched its sweet savour ascending on high,
Accepted, O Father, by Thee.

And lo, while I gazed at the glorious sight,
A voice from above reached mine ears:
'By this thine iniquity's taken away,
And no trace of it on thee appears.'

AMELIA MATILDA HULL 1825-1882

"I COULD NOT ENUMERATE THE TIMES GOD HAS RESCUED MY SOUL FROM DARKNESS AND DISCOURAGEMENT BY THE SINGING OF A HYMN. ALSO I HAVE SEEN VAST AUDIENCES MELTED BY A SIMPLE HYMN WHEN EVERY OTHER INSTRUMENTALITY HAS FAILED."

DR. PENTECOST, PREACHER

Chapter Twenty Three

Horatio Gates Spafford
Who Lost All, But Gave All

H ow would you cope with tragedy? How would you cope with trials and tribulations? How would you cope with a series of calamities?

Surely we are compelled to seek the help and mercy of the Lord, to rely upon Him for comfort and consolation. Though some would dare to question the Almighty in such a situation, not so Horatio Spafford. When wealth and family were taken from him in tragic circumstances, he found peace with God and relied upon His Providential will. He could say with confidence "It is well."

'When peace like a river attendeth my way...'

Spafford was born in New York and spent his early life there. He later removed to Chicago where he became a prosperous business-man and a qualified lawyer. He married Anna Lawson and four daughters were born to the union. He was a religious man and attached himself to the local Presbyterian congregation, in which he became a Sunday School teacher. He also gave of his time and energy to the work of the YMCA.

'Though Satan should buffet, tho' trials should come...'

In 1871 property along the shores of Lake Michigan, in which he had invested heavily, was destroyed by fire. Facing financial ruin, he reassessed his life and resolved to sell what remained of his business and to move to the land where his Saviour had walked. The initial step was for his wife and daughters to travel to Europe where he would join them when legal matters were settled.

'When sorrow, like sea-billows roll...'

The ladies set sail on the American ship "SS Ville du Havre." But on the 22nd November 1873, sailing off the coast of Newfoundland, the vessel collided with the British ship "The Lochearn." Along with many others, the four young girls were drowned; Mrs Spafford was dragged unconscious from the sea. It was a further ten days before the survivors were landed in South Wales. The pathetic telegram to her husband bore the message "Saved alone." Spafford left immediately to join his grief-stricken wife. Their plans now were to return to the USA, to the comfort and fellowship of friends and relatives.

Horatio resumed his legal practice and involved himself in the church activities. His association with the YMCA, brought him into contact with D L Moody and Ira Sankey. During the 1876 Chicago mission they were guests in the Spafford home. Perhaps encouraged by Sankey, Spafford at this time wrote a memorial to his daughters, who - though lost at sea - had each been converted and were found in Christ. The poem 'It is well with my soul' so came to be composed. The music was added by Philip Bliss and he had the privilege of singing the piece for the first time in Farwell Hall, Chicago. Bliss entitled his musical accompaniment "Ville du Havre" and it has been inextricably wedded to the words ever since.

'Whatever my lot...'

In the next few years, three children were born to the Spaffords. Life seemed to have taken a better course. However in 1880, scarlet fever took their only son. The couple now determined to "surrender all" and sold-up and again set sail for the Holy Land, to fulfil the plans so abruptly and tragically halted years before. They became involved in the American community in Palestine and through their labour much medical and spiritual help was liberally dispensed. Their efforts were appreciated and the family were highly regarded by the Arab population. Following Horatio's death, the Spafford Memorial Children's Hospital continued an efficient and effective work in that place.

Horatio Spafford was buried in the Protestant cemetery on Mount Zion, Jerusalem. His soul at rest, but trouble was still to come! In the Arab-Israeli conflict in 1967, Arab soldiers raided the graves of the cemetery, thinking that the graves were Jewish. The remains were thrown into the Hinnom Valley. When the war was over, the skeleton remains were re-interred in a communal grave as it was obviously impossible to identify each individual. A new headstone was erected and Spafford's name is at the top. For one frail American lady, 91 at the time, the re-interment service was a poignant occasion. She was Mrs Bertha Vester, the fifth daughter of the Spaffords; she had spent her life in Jerusalem fulfilling the family desire to serve the Master.

Elisabeth Elliot, the widow of Jim Elliot, one of the martyred missionaries of Ecuador, held a particular affection for Spafford's hymn. She wrote that "To love God, is to love His Will. That which He gives - we receive. That which He takes - we relinquish." Such were Spafford's sentiments, and what spiritual lessons we can learn from the verses of his touching hymn.

"When peace, like a river, attendeth my way,
When sorrows, like sea billows, roll;
Whatever my lot, Thou hast taught me to say,
It is well, it is well with my soul.

My sin - O the bliss of this glorious thought! -
My sin, not in part, but the whole,
Is nailed to His cross, and I bear it no more;
Praise the Lord, praise the Lord, O my soul!

But, Lord, 'tis for Thee, for Thy coming, we wait;
The sky, not the grave, is our goal;
O trump of the angel! O voice of the Lord!
Blessed hope! blessed rest of my soul!"

HORATIO GATES SPAFFORD 1828-1888

"PRAISE IS OUR SOLACE AFTER TRIAL. MUSIC IS SWEETEST WHEN HEARD OVER RIVERS AND BLESSING GOD OVER THE FLOODS OF AFFLICTION, MAKE THE SWEETEST MUSIC IN THE EARS OF HEAVEN."

ANDREW FULLER, BAPTIST THEOLOGIAN

Chapter Twenty Four

SAMUEL TREVOR FRANCIS
AN UNTIRING LABOURER

"The days of our years are threescore years and ten; and if by reason of strength they be fourscore years, yet is their strength labour and sorrow," says the prayer of Moses (Psalm 90 v 10). Trevor Francis not only passed 70 and 80 but 90 and for seventy three of those years he was preaching the Gospel! Born in Cheshunt, the son of an artist whose circumstances dictated that the family move from place to place, young Trevor was brought up in London, moving after some years to Hull, where some form of settled life prevailed. The family attached themselves to the local parish church. The father encouraged his two sons to join him in the choir. Trevor was impressed by the various pieces the choir was required to sing, but sadly their religion was as much a performance as their singing and the ritual substituted for the real thing.

The interest in singing and music was sustained and he began to produce poetry on a variety of subjects. He kept a note-book of his jottings and over a period of time gathered a collection in his own handwriting. When he began employment in London, he endured times of ill-health and soon had to return to relatives in Hull. It was then that he came under the sound of the Gospel and heard Biblical teaching. On one occasion he was invited to attend a baptismal service - he had been told that he would see a man buried alive! - but no inward work was accomplished at that event. His conversion came about in a strange way and occurred when he was back in London.

He was crossing Hungerford Bridge when he was brought to an abrupt halt by some unseen and irresistible force. He heard the question being asked: "Do you believe in the Lord Jesus Christ?" He responded "I believe," and from that moment "old things passed away .... and all things are become new." He did not seek out a parish church but felt at home with the Plymouth Brethren though his broad associations would not be welcome in today's assemblies. When D L Moody began his campaign in London in 1873, Francis proved to be a willing worker. At times he was invited to deputise for Sankey in leading the praise. He also allied himself to Canon Hay Aiken in several of his missions, which were distinguished by the fact that many churchmen were converted.

On his own account he commenced open-air preaching, a ministry he maintained for a remarkable 73 years. He saw many brought to saving faith in Christ in London and elsewhere when he proclaimed the Word of Life. He was mightily used of God during the 1859 Revival and his zeal for evangelism was unabated. Even when his health failed and it was recommended that he travel abroad, he used the opportunity to preach in Canada, Australia, Palestine and Egypt. He had the joy of hearing his own hymns sung in the native tongue whilst on his travels. He accompanied R C Morgan to parts of North Africa - an experience which left a deep impression upon him.

At home the collection of poems written over decades was presented to the public in a volume bearing the title of one of his hymns - 'O the deep, deep love of Jesus'. Commenting on this book Dr Thirtle wrote that all Francis's poetical work as well as his spoken word was permeated by a realisation of the love of Christ. Apart from the title hymn, 'I am waiting for the dawning' still remains in many compilations.

"O the deep, deep love of Jesus!
Vast, unmeasured, boundless, free
Rolling as a mighty ocean,
In its fulness over me.
Underneath me, all around me,
Is the current of Thy love;
Leading onward, leading homeward,
To my glorious rest above."

Trevor Francis died peacefully in his 92nd year to indeed realise
what he had written:

"At home with the Lord, what joy is this!
To gaze on His face in infinite bliss."

SAMUEL TREVOR FRANCIS 1834-1925

"MINISTERS OF SONG TAKE US
TO HEIGHTS OF WHICH
THE SOUL OFTEN DREAMS,
YET RARELY ATTAINS - IN FACT TO
THOSE MANSIONS OF THE BLEST
WHERE THERE ARE ALWAYS LIGHT AND
WARMTH AND LOVE; WHERE THE
THIRST OF WEARY PILGRIMS IS
QUENCHED BY DRAUGHTS OF
MOUNTAIN SPRINGS; AND WHERE
THIS MORTAL SPIRIT PUTS ON
IMMORTALITY."

FANNY J CROSBY

Chapter Twenty Five

SABINE BARING-GOULD
A PROLIFIC AUTHOR AND HUMBLE PREACHER

Wealth and privilege characterised the early life of Baring-Gould. He was born in Exeter and lived on the family estate in South Devon. His father had the means to send his eldest son abroad to travel and to live for a short time in France and Germany. He returned to England to further his education and graduated from Cambridge with a couple of degrees. He kept up his studies until he entered the Anglican ministry in 1864. He began his first charge with enthusiasm and his zeal was soon noticed and a new challenge was presented to him. He became the incumbent of Horbury Bridge in the Calder Valley in Yorkshire, in 1867.

The congregation there was a small gathering of local people and the parish was better described as a mission. His home, a humble cottage with a single room and back kitchen downstairs and another room upstairs, had also to serve as the meeting place. For the pulpit, he had to improvise with a chair set in front of the chimney in the upper room. The meetings attracted increasing attendances and before long the room was filled, then the stairs and finally the ground floor. The people were appreciative of his preaching and enjoyed the conviviality of the place.

It had its drawbacks though. The singing was unimpressive as the music "had to bump down the stairs, fill the kitchen and one strain of the tune after another came up through the chinks in the floor, to interfere with the smoothness and sequence of the melody as sung above!"

During the winter nights, Baring-Gould organised night classes for young and old. Remember that at that time both children and adults did a long days work of twelve hours and more in the woollen mills, yet they came to sit late into the night to be taught by the curate. They learned to read and to write and to count and were encouraged to appreciate poetry and music! Some of the poems were written by the curate and this gave him the opportunity to impart spiritual lessons. He specifically wrote 'Now the day is over' for the night school. The phraseology is noticeably simple, almost child-like in style. It is founded on Proverbs 3 v 24 and originally consisted of a dozen verses.

"Now the day is over,
Night is drawing nigh,
Shadows of the evening
Steal across the sky."

The tune 'Eudoxia' was of his own composition, though he later admitted that it was a remembrance of a German air he had heard many years before!

By far his supreme composition was 'Onward Christian Soldiers', also written in connection with Horbury, but this time for the Sunday School. It was the practise to have a Whit Sunday Procession, complete with brass band and banners. He later explained that he "wanted the children to sing as they marched from one village to another, but I couldn't think of anything suitable. So I sat up at night and resolved that I would have to write something myself, 'Onward Christian Soldiers' was the result. It was written in great haste and I am afraid some of the rhymes are faulty. Certainly nothing has surprised me more than its popularity."

"Onward Christian Soldiers
Marching as to war,
Looking unto Jesus,
Who is gone before:
Christ, the royal Master,
Leads against the foe;
Forward into battle,
See, His banners go!"

Some words and phrases of the hymn have been altered over the years. For example the third and fourth lines of the first verse made reference to the "Cross of Jesus, going on before," but Low-Church colleagues of the writer took exception to symbols and the like. One caustically wrote: "With the Cross of Jesus - left behind the door!" No amount of alteration, however, satisfied D L Moody, who refused to include the hymn in his meetings. He complained that the sentiments "were too much like boasting."

It was during his time at Horbury that he met and fell in love with Grace Taylor, the daughter of a mill labourer. Their different "stations" in life meant that their plans for marriage had to be abated. Baring-Gould never had any doubts about their compatibility, but he suggested a solution to the social difficulty. He persuaded her parents to allow her to attend college to secure an education. The parents agreed and when Grace completed her course the wedding went ahead. They were happily united for almost fifty years till her death in 1916. On her tombstone he had engraved a short inscription: "Half my soul." It was eight years later that Baring-Gould's remains were laid in the same graveyard at Lew Trenchard. He had ministered there in his home parish for forty-three years, since 1881. At the same time he was the local squire.

Throughout his life, from university days on, he was a prolific writer on an infinite variety of subjects. For him writing was a recreation and one to which he expended much energy. He said it was his philosophy to "stick to the task when I begin it. And it would never do to wait from day to day for some moments which might seem favourable for work."

Over a five year period he produced a 15 volume "Lives of the Saints" and had the distinction of having the work placed on the Vatican's list of prohibited reading! He wrote books on mythology and superstition, folklore, history and travel. He published a collection of hymns and carols and several volumes of West Country ballads. He gained a popular following with a series of novels, including a thriller! It was said of him that he had more works attached to his name in the British Museum Catalogue, than any other writer of his time. The Church of Jesus Christ can be grateful for his great and enduring hymn 'Onward Christian Soldiers'.

SABINE BARING-GOULD 1834-1924

"AS THE EVIL SPIRIT IN SAUL YIELDED IN OLDEN TIME TO THE INFLUENCE OF THE HARP, SO WOULD THE SPIRIT OF MELANCOLY OFTEN TAKE FLIGHT FROM US IF ONLY WE WOULD TAKE UP THE SONG OF PRAISE."

PHILIP POWER, MINISTER & AUTHOR

Chapter Twenty Six

KNOWLES SHAW
PASTOR AND COMPOSER

The dying words of Albin Shaw to his son, Knowles, were to be indelibly inscribed on the mind of the young boy. "Be good to your mother and prepare to meet your God"- the words were ever before him, even long past the time of grieving. The family was not blessed with many possessions but one item was particularly treasured. That was father's violin. Knowles demonstrated some skill on the precious instrument and he practised to become as accomplished as its first owner.

As a young man he fulfilled his father's wish and succeeded in providing for his mother, also according her respect and honour as the Scriptures demanded in Exodus 20 verse 12. He was not so diligent in exercising his father's dying desire that he "prepare to meet thy God" (Amos 4 v 12). He employed his musical ability for the entertainment of the world and he became a popular character, much in demand at parties.

On one specific occasion he was playing to an assembled gathering of young revellers, intent upon having a "good time" when he came under conviction of sin. His father's words echoed in his head and he stood before the puzzled crowd unable to play. He knew as never before that he had failed to obey his father's counsel and he was just like the Prodigal Son, seeking satisfaction in the world and finding it all vanity. He prayed for God's forgiveness, just where he stood. Salvation was immediate and he departed the company of revellers and entered the congregation of the Redeemed.

With a new song in his heart, he felt he had a new message to proclaim. He trained for the ministry and went on to become an evangelist and writer. Throughout his ministry he is said to have received over 10,000 people into the church.

Shaw ended his earthly sojourn in circumstances similar to that of Philip Bliss (author of 'I am so glad'). He had completed an evangelistic campaign in Dallas, Texas and had boarded the train to return home to his family in Columbus, Mississippi. On route the locomotive was derailed and many passengers were injured. The preacher was entangled in the wreckage but died from his injuries before rescuers could extricate him. His dying words to those accompanying him were recorded thus: "It is a grand thing to rally people to the Cross of Christ."

His hymns still achieve that object, especially 'Sowing in the morning' which is sung across the world in countless Gospel meetings, and is recognised as typical of Revivalist songs. Shaw had taken Psalm 126 verses 5 & 6 as the theme for this hymn. "They that sow in tears shall reap in joy. He that goeth forth and weepeth shall doubtless come again with rejoicing, bringing his sheaves with him."

"Sowing in the morning, sowing seeds of kindness,
Sowing in the noontide, and the dewy eves,
Waiting for the harvest, and the time of reaping:
We shall come rejoicing, bringing in the sheaves.

Go then ever weeping, sowing for the Master,
Though the loss sustained our spirit often grieves;
When our weeping's over, He will bid us welcome:
We shall come rejoicing, bringing in the sheaves."

Only Eternity will reveal the sheaves gathered through the ministry of Shaw's great hymn.

KNOWLES SHAW BORN 1834

Chapter Twenty Seven

WILLIAM JAMES KIRKPATRICK

IRISH IMMIGRANT WHO BECAME A COMPOSER

You can hardly repeat the words 'Away in a manger', without being aware of the music associated with it. The tune is 'Cradle Song' and the composer was William James Kirkpatrick. His music is attached to a number of well-known hymns, such as 'Will your anchor hold', 'Life at best is very brief', 'O spread the tidings round', and 'King of my life, I crown Thee now'. He was a close friend of Fanny J Crosby, to whom he often dispatched melodies for her to add suitable words. This was the case with the accompaniment for 'He hideth my soul' and 'Redeemed, how I love to proclaim it'. In her autobiography in 1906, Miss Crosby commented that she had written hundreds of hymns for Kirkpatrick.

While most of his days were lived in the USA, Kirkpatrick was in fact born and brought up in Duncannon, near to Waterford in Southern Ireland. The family emigrated in the time of the Famine and settled in Pennsylvania. As a youth he took an interest in music and gained some expertise on the flute and also the violin. He joined A S Jenks in collecting camp-meeting songs and they produced an amazing 47 volumes. This did not secure a career for him and so for a few years he worked as a carpenter. During the Civil War he served as principal musician and fife major of the 91st Pennsylvania Volunteers, but was later deployed to work as a ship-builder until the close of the war.

In peacetime, Kirkpatrick was connected with a furniture manufacturer, but in 1878 he abandoned business and devoted his time and talent to the writing of hymns and choruses and sacred music. Perhaps his best known piece, for which he wrote both words and melody is 'I've wandered far away from God'. This is based on the Parable of the Prodigal Son (Luke 15). It has been sung as an invitation hymn in evangelistic services for generations. It would be impossible to calculate the number of souls touched by the sentiments of his hymn.

"I've wandered far away from God:
Now I'm coming home;
The paths of sin too long I've trod:
Lord I'm coming home.

I'm tired of sin and straying, Lord:
Now I'm coming home;
I'll trust Thy love, believe Thy Word:
Lord, I'm coming home."

His tunes for 'He hideth my soul' (Crosby) he called 'Kirkpatrick' and for 'Lead me to Calvary' (Hussey) he named 'Duncannon' after his birth-place.

Kirkpatrick passed into the Lord's presence while resting in his favourite armchair. At his feet lay a piece of paper on which he had written:

'Just as Thou wilt, Lord, this is my cry
Just as thou wilt, to live or to die,
I am Thy servant; Thou knowest best:
Just as Thou wilt, Lord, labour or rest.

WILLIAM JAMES KIRKPATRICK

Just as Thou wilt, Lord, - which shall it be,
Life everlasting waiting for me,
Or shall I tarry here at Thy feet?
Just as Thou wilt, Lord, whatever is meet.'

George C Stebbins, a fellow composer, wrote of Kirkpatrick's
dying testimony:
"To voice such words of resignation, then to close his eyes and
open them again in a moment's time, is as striking and impressive as
it is beautiful. What an awakening he must have had! Well might
every child of God covet such an ending of his life."

WILLIAM JAMES KIRKPATRICK 1838-1921

"IT IS SCARCELY POSSIBLE TO
EXAGGERATE THE INFLUENCE OF
HYMNS. THEY HAVE PROBABLY
DONE AS MUCH TO KEEP ALIVE IN THE
CHURCH THE 'FAITH WHICH WAS
ONCE DELIVERED UNTO THE SAINTS'
AS ALL THE CREEDS."

REV DUNCAN CAMPBELL, MINISTER & AUTHOR

Chapter Twenty Eight

WILLIAM PATON MACKAY
DOCTOR, PREACHER AND WRITER

" **T**he older I grew, the more wicked I became. For the God of my mother - I did not care in the least, but rather sought by all means to drive Him out of my thoughts. I was in danger of becoming a thorough infidel, but for the voice of my conscience ever accusing and reproaching me," so begins the testimony of William Mackay.

Mackay had been brought up in a Godly home and was no stranger to the Gospel. He had witnessed the precious fruit, produced alone by the Christian faith, in the life of his mother. She had prayed for his soul's salvation but the rebellious young man had his own plans. Through application and diligent study he achieved his ambition to be a physician, but an incident at the hospital, where he had been appointed, was to change his future forever.

Mackay has left a brief record of what happened on that significant day. An injured labourer, who had fallen a considerable height on a building site, was brought into his hospital. It was unfortunately all too obvious that the man's plight was hopeless and all that could be done was to comfort him and alleviate his pain. The patient feebly enquired of Mackay as to how long he would last. The doctor gave his opinion in a cautious and sympathetic manner.

"I went to see him on my regular visits. What struck me most was the quiet, almost happy, expression which was constantly on his face. I knew he was a Christian, but about such matters I cared not to talk with him or hear."

After the man died, some things regarding his affairs were to be attended to and his possessions had to be disposed of, as he had no relatives. The nurse, holding a book in her hand, enquired: "What will we do with this?" The book was a Bible; it had been well used, many pages were loose, others torn and the cover damaged. "I took the Bible and - could I believe my eyes? It was my own Bible! The Bible which my mother had given me when I left my parent's home, and which later, when short of money, I had sold for a small amount. Yes, I had sold it. My name was still in it, written in my mother's own hand, and beneath it the verse she had selected for me. I stood as if in a dream, but I regained my self-control, managing to conceal before those present my deep emotion. In seemingly indifferent manner and tone I answered the nurse: 'The Book is old and has hardly any value, let me keep it and I will see about the rest'. "

While looking through the book, he read again those precious verses which he had heard in his youth. The regained possession was the means of his conversion. The voice of his conscience could no longer be silenced. He was enabled to believe, by God's grace and mercy, that "Christ Jesus came into the world to save sinners." (1 Tim.1:15) So in this unique way, the prayers of so many years previously were answered.

For a while Mackay maintained his medical career, but he felt the Lord's leading to bring the Gospel to needy souls. Professor, later Sir, James Y Simpson (who discovered chloroform) recognised the young doctor's aptitude for preaching and he encouraged him to exercise his abilities in that direction. His evangelistic endeavours led to a number of calls being presented to him to become the pastor of churches both large and small. He accepted a call signed by just over twenty people to be the minister of a Presbyterian congregation in Hull. Under his charge the smallest and the weakest congregation was built into a large and thriving witness. There he remained refusing other appeals.

He was noted for his energy and zeal, and he had strong individualistic views. For example, during his pastorate in Hull he would not accept a fixed income from the church. Instead he relied upon the contributions voluntarily placed in a box in the lobby of the church. Mackay was in great demand as a conference speaker throughout the British Isles and the USA, and he supported D L Moody in London and Edinburgh at the time of his great campaigns. He compiled his own evangelistic addresses into three volumes: 'Grace and Truth', 'Abundant Grace' and 'The Seeking Saviour'. Of the first volume, C H Spurgeon commented that it was "full of Gospel Truth - dripping with it like the honeycomb with honey."

Mackay had a holiday home built in Oban in his native Scotland, to where he resorted when a break from his labours permitted. On one such visit while boarding the ferry, he tripped striking his head and falling into the sea. He was not to recover and within two days passed into the presence of the Lord. His permanent memorial is his series of sermons and some hymns including 'Worthy, Worthy' and 'We praise thee, O God, for the son of Thy love'.

"Worthy, worthy is the Lamb,
Worthy, worthy is the Lamb,
Worthy, worthy is the Lamb,
That was slain.

Praise Him, Hallelujah!
Praise Him, Hallelujah!
Praise Him, Hallelujah!
Praise the Lamb

We the crown of life shall wear,
We the palm of victory wear,
All our Father's blessings share
In the Lamb.

And when landed safe above
In the kingdom of His love,
We shall the fulness prove
Of the Lamb."

WILLIAM PATON MACKAY 1839-1885

"THERE IS NO HEAVEN, EITHER IN THIS WORLD OR THE WORLD TO COME, FOR PEOPLE WHO DO NOT PRAISE GOD. IF THEY DO NOT ENTER INTO THE SPIRIT OF HEAVEN, HOW CAN THE SPIRIT AND JOY OF HEAVEN ENTER INTO THEM."

DR. PULSFORD, MINISTER & AUTHOR

Chapter Twenty Nine

ELISHA ALBRIGHT HOFFMAN
AUTHOR OF HYMNS WITH QUESTIONS

Wherever the Gospel has been faithfully preached, it is almost certain that one of Hoffman's hymns will also be sung. The simple yet direct 'Have you been to Jesus for the cleansing power?' has been a challenge to many a concerned soul. Likewise 'Where will you spend Eternity?' and 'Will you be ready when the Bridegroom comes?' Hoffman had a wonderful faculty for articulating the Gospel appeal in but a few and memorable lines.

His unique talent was employed by the Rev Anthony Showalter who sent him a tune and a chorus and requested that he attach suitable words which would compliment both. The chorus, which was based on Deuteronomy 33 verse 27, was:

'Leaning, leaning, safe and secure from all alarms
Leaning, leaning, leaning on the Everlasting Arms.'

Hoffman obliged with the words of 'What a fellowship, what a joy divine'. The joint effort proved to be a satisfactory combination, and on the occasion of the first rendition in Showalter's church, many people came to know the Saviour.

Elisha Hoffman was a son of the manse and he always dreamed of following his father's footsteps. Hoffman (senior) was a preacher of the Gospel, an evangelical and an evangelist. Elisha knew that his intended career was not an automatic procedure, but when he was soundly converted, he felt the call of God to bring the Good News to others. At the age of 27 he was licensed to preach and he also accepted responsibility as assistant editor of a religious publication called 'The Living Epistle'. Many of his hymns were to appear in its columns.

In 1876 he published a collection of children's hymns and choruses entitled 'Happy Songs for Sunday School'. Included in that compilation were 'Down at the Cross', (with the chorus 'Glory to His Name'), and 'What a Wonderful Saviour'. Hoffman little realised how enduring his collection would prove.

His hymn 'I must tell Jesus all of my troubles' was the outcome of a conversation with one of his parishioners, a lady who had suffered more than a fair share of life's problems. She had pleaded for his help with the appeal : "What must I do?" Relying on 1 John 1 verse 7, Hoffman replied, "You must tell Jesus all." He records that "The woman seemed abstracted in meditation, then her face glowed, her eyes lighted up and with animation she exclaimed 'Yes, I must tell Jesus.' As I went from that sorrow-filled home a vision walked before me of a soul transformed from darkness into light." Upon returning to his home he wrote both the words and music of the hymn, based on the woman's joyous cry.

Hoffman's earthly ministry ended in his ninetieth year, but his hymns and choruses live on, to be sung and enjoyed by successive generations.

"Have you been to Jesus for the cleansing power?
Are you washed in the blood of the Lamb?
Are you fully trusting in His grace this hour?
Are you washed in the blood of the lamb?

ELISHA ALBRIGHT HOFFMAN

Are you washed in the blood,
In the soul cleansing blood of the Lamb?
Are your garments spotless? are they white as snow?
Are you washed in the blood of the Lamb?

Are you daily walking by the Saviour's side?
Are you washed in the blood of the Lamb?
Do you rest each moment in the Crucified?
Are you washed in the blood of the Lamb?

ELISHA ALBRIGHT HOFFMAN 1839-1929

"**I**T IS UNFORTUNATE THAT MANY MUSICIANS AND THEOLOGIANS LOOK DOWN ON THE GOSPEL SONG AS IF IT WERE NOT QUITE CLASSIC ENOUGH. THERE ARE MANY THINGS TO COMMEND THE GOSPEL SONG - ESPECIALLY THE REPETITION OF THE CHORUS FOR EMPHASIS."

JOHN R RICE, EVANGELIST & WRITER

Chapter Thirty

DANIEL WEBSTER WHITTLE
SOLDIER, SINGER AND SOUL-WINNER

When the American Civil War broke out, countless young men enlisted in the opposing armies of the Union and the Confederacy. Daniel Whittle left his home in New England to serve as a lieutenant in the Massachusetts regiment of the Union army. He came from a godly home but like so many of his age, he rebelled against the claims of Christ and sought to face the world in his own strength. He was to learn a tragic and lifelong lesson when in one military encounter, at the Battle of Vicksburg, he was severely injured and in a crude field-hospital had an arm amputated.

His recovery was slow and the surroundings void of the action he longed to engage in. Bored with his plight and rummaging in his haversack intent on organising his belongings, he discovered a New Testament - the one which his mother had given him and the one he had promised to read.

"I read right through the Book, every part was interesting to me. I found to my surprise that I could understand it in a way that I never had before. I read it through again and for days I continued reading!"

He still had no thought of Salvation but something was to bring about a change. One night his usual reading was interrupted by a nurse seeking his help to pray for a fellow patient. Whittle honestly replied that he had never really prayed in his life and there was not much he could do now. The nurse had assumed from his frequent Bible study that he must be a praying man - she persisted with her plea. Whittle finally agreed to accompany the nurse to the dying soldier.

In his weakness the young man told Whittle that he had been brought up in a Godly home and had gone to Sunday School, but life as a soldier had deepened him in sin. Now in his hour of need, he had nothing to rely on for Eternity. It all sounded too familiar to Whittle! "Pray for me. Ask God to forgive me. Ask Christ to save me!" he pleaded.

"As I stood there God said to my soul - just as plainly as if He had spoken in audible tones - 'You know the way of salvation, get down on your knees and accept Christ, and then pray for this boy'."

There and then he confessed his sins and asked God for Christ's sake to forgive him.

"I believed right there that He did forgive me, and that I was Christ's child. I then prayed earnestly for the boy. He became quiet, and pressed my hand as I pleaded the promises. When I arose from my knees he was dead. I can but believe that God, who used him to bring me to my Saviour, used me to get his attention fixed upon Him."

Whittle knew that the army was no longer his life especially with his disability. He was discharged with the rank of major and began another campaign - to win souls for Christ. He graphically illustrated his evangelistic messages with accounts of his military career. On one such occasion he recounted the story of General Hood and his Confederate Army storming the Union garrison at Altoona Pass: when almost at the point of defeat, the Union soldiers sighted a flag signal in the distance - "Hold the fort, I am coming. Sherman." (Whittle had served for a time as a captain under General Sherman). Philip Bliss was in the audience and took the words of Sherman to write the hymn beginning 'Hold the fort, for I am coming, Jesus beckons still'.

For almost ten years the Whittle and Bliss partnership arranged Gospel campaigns across the States. The Major was also a prolific hymn-writer and with Bliss had the responsibility of producing Sankey's book 'Gospel Hymns and Sacred Songs'. Henry Varley, the evangelist, let it be known that he took exception to Annie Sherwood Hawk's hymn 'I need Thee every hour'. He complained to Whittle that he felt the sentiments to be unsatisfactory, because he needed Christ every moment not just every hour. Pedantic perhaps, but the remark encouraged Whittle to write: 'Dying with Jesus, by death reckoned mine'. The chorus surely was pleasing to Varley - 'Moment by moment'. Incidentally, the music for this hymn was composed by Whittle's daughter May who married Will Moody, one of the sons of D L Moody.

Whittle was associated with Moody in his evangelistic campaigns, and helped with the preaching as well as providing Sankey with hymns to sing. When Moody visited Belfast, Whittle also preached at several meetings including one at Crumlin Road prison.

Among Whittle's compositions are 'Redemption Ground, the ground of peace', 'Have you any room for Jesus?', 'There's a royal banner', 'There shall be showers of blessing' and 'I know Whom I have believed'. Some pieces appeared under his pseudonym 'El Nathan'.

"I know not why God's wondrous grace
To me has been made known,
Nor why - unworthy as I am -
He claimed me for His own.

But 'I know whom I have believed,
and am persuaded - that He is able
to keep that which I've committed
unto Him against that day.

I know not how the Spirit moves,
Convincing men of sin,
Revealing Jesus through the Word,
Creating faith in him.

I know not when my Lord shall come;
I know not how, nor where;
If I shall pass the vale of death,
Or meet Him in the air."

DANIEL WEBSTER WHITTLE 1840-1901

"SING OF YOUR GLORIOUS HOPES, AND LET THE ENEMY HEAR NO DESPONDING OR DOUBTING NOTE. SING OF YOUR FUTURE AND OF THE ENDLESS REIGN OF YOUR LIFE IN CHRIST JESUS. MAKE A JOYFUL NOISE IN YOUR HEARTS AND YOUR ASSEMBLIES TO YOUR GREAT UNCHANGEABLE FATHER."

DR. PULSFORD, MINISTER & AUTHOR

Chapter Thirty One

IrA DaviD SankeY
INTERNATIONAL SINGER AND EVANGELIST

D L Moody had a distinct disadvantage when it came to
congregational singing - he was tone deaf! Of course, he
appreciated the importance of music in Christian worship
and to that end he had approached two well-known singers (Philip
Phillips and Philip Bliss) to help him in his evangelistic campaigns.
Both men had other commitments and so the search went on for the
right man.

So it happened that when Ira Sankey was asked to lead the praise
at a dull YMCA convention in July 1870, Moody knew that he had
found a new song leader! Introduced after the meeting Sankey was
asked, "What do you do for a living?" "In government service," he
replied. "Well you'll have to give that up and come to Chicago to
work with me, I've been looking for the likes of you for eight years!"
In fact it was six months later before Sankey was convinced that he
should resign as a tax inspector and to commence full-time work
with Moody. A thirty year harmonious association with the great
evangelist had now begun.

Ira Sankey was born in Edinburgh, Pennsylvania of English and
Scots-Irish stock. The family was prosperous and his father held a

135

position in the Pennsylvanian Legislature. The Sankeys worshipped at the local Methodist church and it was during a Gospel crusade in 1855 that Ira came under conviction of sin and called unto the Lord for Salvation. He soon became involved in the work of the church and within five years he was appointed Sunday School superintendent. He also employed his rich baritone voice in the worship services.

When Civil War enveloped the USA, Ira enrolled in the Union Army. He did not distinguish himself as a military man, though on one occasion his voice saved his life! It was not until some years after the war that he heard, that when he was on sentry duty and he had begun to sing to while away the time, a southern soldier had him in the sights of his sniper rifle. The confederate was touched by the beautiful singing and was unable to pull the trigger.

The Moody-Sankey partnership brought them across the Atlantic to the British Isles. They were announced thus: "Moody will preach the Gospel; Sankey will sing the Gospel." It was always the singer's purpose to select a hymn compatible with the preacher's message. At a convention in Edinburgh (Scotland) Dr Horatius Bonar was the final speaker and his theme was the Good Shepherd. Moody, acting as chairman for a change, asked Sankey to bring a suitable solo, but the 23rd Psalm had already been sung.

Sankey recalled that he had kept a newspaper cutting of a poem he had read the previous day. He produced it from his pocket and took his place at the organ. Imagine the situation, a poem that he had never sung before - and with no music composed for it! Not only the congregation sat in expectation! Sankey wrote of the experience:-

"I struck the chord of A flat and began to sing. Note by note the tune was given and it has not been changed from that day to this. At the end of the first verse, a difficulty presented itself to me. Could I accurately repeat the music I had just played? I lifted up my heart in prayer and was able to remember."

The poem was entitled 'The Lost Sheep' by Elizabeth Clephane. We know it as 'There were ninety and nine' and that was how the music came to be written. In less stressful circumstances, Sankey composed the music for countless sacred pieces. He wrote the tunes for 'Beneath the Cross of Jesus', 'O safe to the Rock', 'I am Redeemed', 'Simply trusting', 'Under His Wings', 'It passeth knowledge', 'Faith is the Victory', and 'Am I a soldier of the Cross', to name but a few!

In 1873 the 'Moody-Sankey Hymnbook' appeared; this was a mere 16 page pamphlet of words and music. A later edition had words only and the British royalties from sales yielded sufficient funds to complete the construction of Moody's Chicago church. Subsequent additions to the book culminated in the 1200 piece 'Sacred Songs and Solos'.

When Moody died in December 1899, Sankey continued campaigning as an evangelist and singer. However by 1902 fatigue forced him to retire.

Unable to remain idle, he embarked upon a revision of his hymnbook. Sadly this had to be abandoned when glaucoma robbed him of his eyesight. He passed into Eternity 13th August 1908 to sing a New Song.

"Behold a Fountain deep and wide,
Behold its onward flow;
'Twas opened in the Saviour's side
And cleaneth white as snow.

Come to this Fountain!
'Tis flowing today;
And all who will may freely come
And wash their sins away.

From Calvary's cross, where Jesus died
In sorrow, pain and woe,
Burst forth the wondrous crimson tide
That cleanseth white as snow."

IRA DAVID SANKEY 1840-1908

Chapter Thirty Two

EDWARD UFFORD
REMEMBERED FOR HIS NAUTICAL HYMN

E dward Ufford has given us a hymn on a nautical theme which is unsurpassed. His 'Throw out the life-line' when sung at a slow rather than a bracing pace, as is common today, evokes a tremendous sympathetic emotion. This was the intended purpose of the composition. The hymn came to be written when Ufford was the pastor of the Baptist Church in Westwood, near to Boston, USA. The small town was on the eastern seaboard and looking out of the manse, at low tide, the remains of an old wreck embedded in the sands could be seen.

"As I trod the shore and seeing the old wreck my imagination strove to picture what the storm did on the fateful night when it tossed the craft ashore, where it was soon dashed to pieces," Ufford recalled some years later. These thoughts encouraged him to hold an open-air Gospel meeting to warn "all those who might pass by of their danger." Many did gather to hear him declare the Saviour, the Mighty to save. He was persuaded that the Lord would have him undertake some activity that would make a permanent declaration.

Once again he contemplated the scene of the wreckage. "In my mind's eye I could see a storm and a shipwrecked sailor drifting out beyond human reach. Taking a sheet of paper I wrote the four verses of the hymn. They came as if by inspiration." He also composed the tune which is uniquely attached to it, and so it was published in the autumn of 1886.

Edward Ufford was born in Newark in 1851. The family were a God-fearing people and their service to the Lord's work was a ministry of singing. His father and grandfather had been choir leaders and as a young man he had been trained as a singer. He was converted to Christ as a young man at a time when news of D L Moody's campaigns were being widely reported. The spiritual revival throughout the USA made an impression upon him and he determined to devote his life to the ministry of the Gospel. He sustained a faithful ministry in small pastorates for many years. However, when the popularity of his hymn spread, he became much in demand to both speak and sing at Missionary rallies and Soul-winning conventions. Thus the training in his youth was not fully exercised till his middle years.

In 1902 he embarked upon a world tour and he found that his famous hymn proved to be a "passport" wherever he went! 'Throw out the lifeline' was translated into many languages and as he travelled from place to place, Ufford was complemented for his composition. He had the privilege of seeing the fruit of his endeavour with many souls grasping the Gospel life-line. He continued his service for the Master almost till his eightieth year. The singing of his hymn still performs the writer's intention to alert and to rescue the perishing.

"Throw out the life-line across the dark wave,
There is a brother whom someone should save;
Somebody's brother! O who then will dare
To throw out the life-line, his peril to share?

Soon will the season of rescue be o'er,
Soon will they drift to eternity's shore;
Haste, then, my brother! no time for delay,
But throw out the life-line, and save them today."

EDWARD UFFORD 1851-1930

Chapter Thirty Three

ELIZA EDMUNDS HEWITT
THE SYMPATHETIC POET

Miss Hewitt ranks among the foremost writers of popular hymns. She never left an account of the reasons behind the writing of her sacred compositions, but we know at least that she had a sensitive personality and a compassionate heart. These characteristics must surely have been influential in the publication of 'Christmas with Jesus'. This was intended to be a private poem for a devastated mother whose son had passed away, but the verses were circulated for the benefit of others.

"Christmas in the Father's house,
His first Christmas there;
All the many mansions shining
In the light most fair.
All the golden harp strings ringing
All the angel voices singing
That bright anthem, once again
Which they sang o'er Bethlehem's plain."

Eliza's parents, James and Zeruiah, were a godly couple who determined to raise their children in the ways of truth and righteousness. The family altar was maintained and Scripture and hymn memorisation was encouraged. Eliza placed her trust in the Saviour, early in life, and this was to be a foundation upon which she could - and later circumstances proved that she would - depend. She embarked on a teaching career but a serious accident causing spinal injury ended full-time employment. Whenever her health allowed she engaged in some form of Christian service. She particularly enjoyed the times when she could meet her Sunday School class in the Philadelphia church, where the family worshipped.

Her lifestyle was restricted but she used her enforced invalidity as an opportunity to study God's Word, to pray and to write. She composed a prayer which she said was the true expression of her heart - 'More about Jesus'. She had learned the lesson that when there is more of Jesus, there is less of self and less of the temporal. The prayer/poem was forwarded to John R Sweney to attach suitable music to it, so that others could share its comforting words. His music proved to be the ideal sympathetic melody which her poem required.

The queen of hymn writers, Fanny J Crosby paid Miss Hewitt the following compliment - "she wins the affectionate regard of all who come to know her, and some of her hymns, I am sure, like 'There is sunshine in my soul', 'Never alone', 'Sweeter as the days go by', and 'When we all get to Heaven', will never die." As her own personal favourite Miss Crosby named 'Will there be any stars in my crown.'

"I am thinking today of that beautiful land
I shall reach when the sun goeth down;
When through wonderful grace by my Saviour I stand,
Will there be any stars in my crown.

O what joy will it be when His face I behold,
Living gems at his feet to lay down;
It would sweeten my bliss in the city of gold,
Should there be any stars in my crown."

ELIZA EDMUNDS HEWITT

We can confidently add to the list of Miss Crosby the following enduring pieces: 'Give Me thy heart', 'A trembling soul, I sought the Lord' and 'Once my way was dark and dreary'.

What are the qualities that preserve these hymns? Surely it was Miss Hewitt's sincerity, simplicity of expression and her spiritual insight. She bore her illness with fortitude, and that too spoke of the Saviour's work in her life. A lesson for us all!

ELIZA EDMUNDS HEWITT 1851-1920

"THE HOMAGE THAT WE OWE ALMIGHTY GOD CALLS FOR THE NOBLEST AND MOST REVERENTIAL TRIBUTE THAT MUSIC CAN RENDER."

THOMAS HASTINGS, COMPOSER

Chapter Thirty Four

CHARLES HUTCHINSON GABRIEL
THE KING OF GOSPEL HYMN WRITERS

C harles Alexander was an American singer and evangelist who campaigned with Dr R A Torrey. It was evident that when he rose to sing, he had not just a hymn but a message to deliver. This was particularly the case when he sang 'When all my labours and trials are o'er'. The hymn was eminently suited to his rich tenor voice and it became an essential piece in his vast repertoire. He was thus indebted to his fellow American Charles Gabriel whose composition became popularly known as 'The Glory Song'. Alexander placed the piece first in his 'Revival Hymns' and included it in every edition of the 'Alexander Hymnals'.

The hymn came to be written using the remarks made by an old saint, Ed Card (the Superintendent of the Sunshine Rescue Mission) who often exclaimed "glory" in spontaneous praise during church prayer times. The same character invariably would end his public prayers with "and that will be glory for me." Gabriel took the expression as his theme and published the completed work in 1900 to the amused delight of Card. Within five years the song was being sung around the world, due in most part to Alexander. In his lifetime, 20 million copies of the 'Glory Song' were sold, with translations into 24 languages.

Gabriel was a prolific writer, musician, teacher and publisher. He was responsible for editing over a hundred books of songs, choruses, anthems and cantatas, plus numerous books on musical instruction. For thirty years he was associated with the Homer Rodeheaver Publishing company. The title "The King of Gospel Hymn Writers" was well deserved. The achievement was remarkable considering that he was born and bred in a shanty cabin in Ohio.

In his youth the "music" of the wind and the singing of the birds held a fascination that was to develop and to become an obsession and eventually his life's work. He once rode ten miles - when just a child - to observe and listen to a melodeon being played. He described the experience thus: "no music since then sounded to me more divine."

By his mid-twenties he was sufficiently accomplished to teach music and he also began to compose. He was a powerful tenor singer and was able to arrange his music particularly for that voice. In not so many years he had earned a reputation for quality productions and he was associated with American evangelists Sam Jones and Billy Sunday.

He defined what he believed constituted an acceptable Gospel song:- "First, the text must be systematically constructed, be spiritual and devotional ... begun with an immediate declaration of Truth, presented in a logical and intelligent manner." He also maintained that "Gospel music is the language of the heart; it is both sermon and song, praise and prayer."

He employed his own formula well in 'Send the Light', 'O sweet is the story of Jesus', 'In loving kindness Jesus came', 'I stand amazed in the presence' and 'Sweet is the promise'. He was also responsible for the tunes of 'Higher Ground', 'The way of the Cross leads home' and 'Since Jesus came into my heart' etc. As a publisher he can be credited with the circulation of James M Black's 'When the Roll is called up yonder'. Many well known hymns were improved by his modifications.

CHARLES HUTCHINSON GABRIEL

C H Gabriel died at the home of his son in Hollywood, California, for him the theme of his 'Glory Song' is more precious to its author than ever before:

"When all my labours and trials are o'er
And I am safe on that beautiful shore,
Just to be near the dear Lord I adore,
Will through the ages be glory for me.

O, that will be, glory for me,
Glory for me, glory for me,
When by His grace I shall look on His face,
That will be glory, be glory for me!"

CHARLES HUTCHINSON GABRIEL 1856-1932

"I WOULD RATHER HAVE WRITTEN ONE OF WESLEY'S HYMNS THAN TO HAVE THE FAME OF ALL THE KINGS THAT EVER SAT ON EARTH."

HENRY WARD BEECHER, PREACHER

Chapter Thirty Five

WILLIAM YOUNG
FULLERTON

THE BELFAST MAN WHO WAS SPURGEON'S
FRIEND

D r Fullerton was a man of many talents and inspiring energy: an evangelist, biographer, Keswick speaker, missionary secretary, lecturer etc. In his spare time his hobby was mountaineering!

Born in Belfast, 8 March 1857, he lived at what is now Bradbury Place. The number of the house was 121; in later life he recalled the memories of the home and the blessings of Psalm 121, in both he had found peace and comfort. In 1860 the domestic calm was shattered when his father died as the result of an accident. The family's grief was borne with fortitude and the mother's strong faith maintained a stability that may otherwise have been lacking. His mother kept on part of the family business and until her death had the concession from the Penryhn quarries for supplying Bangor-blue slates to the city!

They worshipped in Fisherwick Presbyterian Church (which was located at what is now the Assembly Buildings) and there the Gospel was faithfully proclaimed by such as Dr John Morgan and

Rev H M Williamson. William heard that he needed to be born-again but his own attempts at self reformation and holy living came to nothing and often provoked tears of disappointment. He wrote of his experiences:

"I wept because of my sins, I wept before God, but it was to no avail. Then came that wonderful Sunday when the new minister spoke to the Sunday School. 'All you have to do to be saved is to take God's gift, and say Thank-you'. Simply and quietly I took the gift for which I have been trying to say Thank-you ever since. On the 20th July 1870 I rested on the infallible Word of God and entered into eternal peace."

He also commented that he was a witness to the fact that a boy of thirteen could have a spiritual experience and an enduring conversion. At another time, Fullerton put it this way:

"On 18th July 1870, the Pope declared himself infallible. On 19th July 1870, France went to war with Germany. On 20th July 1870, I rested on the infallible Word of God for my Salvation. Of these three events, the third to me was the greatest!"

Four years later, D L Moody came to Belfast and this was to be a turning point in the life of the teenage Fullerton. Moody preached a sermon in Rosemary Street Church on "No difference"- many souls responded to the Gospel appeal.

"It never occurred to me to do anything other than to speak to some of those seeking souls. What an apprenticeship it was! What rapture filled my heart, as God used me again and again as people stepped out into the light."

From then on, he knew that it was his business to serve the Lord in pointing men and women to the Saviour. By the time that Moody's Belfast mission had concluded, Fullerton was engaged in three cottage meetings round the city. He began to "bring a word" himself. His efforts were somewhat raw, but so ripe was the harvest that even the "most bungling swing of the scythe seemed to mow down sheaves of ripened grain."

By this time he had completed a five year apprenticeship in the linen trade at a mill at Broadway. He believed in his heart that the Lord would use him in His service and so he travelled to London where he attended Spurgeon's College. He became a member of a local Presbyterian congregation but, like Noah's dove, failed to find a resting place! He did settle, after a time, at the Metropolitan Tabernacle, thus beginning a fifteen year friendship with the Prince of Preachers. Fullerton took charge of several missions in London and soon the raw preacher was ably wielding the scythe! He was trusted with the pulpit of the Metropolitan Tabernacle on dozens of occasions, sometimes substituting for the great preacher, even at short notice.

Following Spurgeon's death, he was permitted to revise his sermons for publication; this meant both editing and enlarging so that the twelve page format was filled. He wrote a biography of C H Spurgeon but he was criticised for taking a non-committal attitude towards the Downgrade Controversy.

Fullerton was also associated with F B Meyer, for whom he conducted a two-month mission in Leicester, in 1884. This campaign was "trebly memorable" not only for the impact of the preaching, but he met the one who was to become his wife and he began an association with Melbourne Hall. He was to return there ten years later as the pastor, a position he held for eighteen years. Thereafter he was appointed Home secretary of the Baptist Missionary Society. This required deputation work at home and sometimes adventurous travels abroad.

Whatever Fullerton's talents were, he was always a "preacher of the Word" and Gospel campaigns were his forte. His meetings would invariably conclude with a great chorus by Major Whittle:

"I will, I will, God helping me,
I will, O Lord, be Thine
Thy precious blood was shed to pardon me,
I will be wholly Thine."

Fullerton earnestly believed that this chorus had a significant impact upon thousands of souls. His own compositions - whether the printed sermons or his wonderful hymn, must also have inestimable results. What better accompaniment could there be for this hymn than the 'Londonderry Air', a fitting compliment for this Ulsterman.

"I cannot tell why He whom angels worship,
Should set His love upon the sons of men,
Or why, as Shepherd, He should seek the wanderers,
To bring them back, they know not how or when.
But this I know, that He was of Mary,
When Bethlehem's manger was His only home,
And that He lived at Nazareth and laboured,
And so the Saviour, Saviour of the world, is come."

WILLIAM YOUNG FULLERTON 1857-1932

"WE SHOULD BE ALWAYS WEARING THE GARMENT OF PRAISE, NOT JUST WAVING A PALM-BRANCH NOW AND THEN."

ANDREW BONAR, PREACHER & AUTHOR

Chapter Thirty Six

ADA RUTH HABERSHON
A WOMAN OF RARE TALENT

F ew women have made a contribution to the cause of Biblical studies equal to that of Miss Habershon. She was the youngest daughter of Dr S O Habershon, of London, where she spent the greater part of her life. Brought up in a Christian home with believing parents, she was early led by God's Grace to believe in the Saviour's love, and her whole life was devoted to His Service.

After formal Bible training she applied herself to a detailed and methodical exploration of the Scriptures. She became an able speaker and lecturer, and an accomplished writer upon the Word of God. She fellowshipped with C H Spurgeon and D L Moody, at whose invitation she toured the USA to lecture on the Old Testament. Her researches were published in several books including the Study series on the Types, Miracles and Parables, plus the 'Outline Study of the Tabernacle'.

She befriended Moody and Sankey when they visited London in 1884. Her support for their mission was publicly acknowledged and she was invited to sing with Sankey and also George C Stebbins, the composer of many popular hymns.

It was not until 1901 that she attempted to write sacred poetry. She relates that on one particular occasion when sickness had limited her otherwise active life, her mind was filled with sweet cheerful thoughts and in a strange way words began to arrange themselves in verse. She considered the Transfiguration and of how the disciples had been led away from busy work to climb mountains with the Master, and the whole scene formed a picture which she described in 'Apart from Him'.

From that time she went on to compose hundreds of songs in response to the "promptings of the Spirit in the ministry of sacred song." During the Torrey-Alexander Mission in London in 1905, she volunteered one of her compositions as a suitable item for Charles Alexander's repertoire. A ready acceptance of her song commenced a stream of over 200 hymns for the American singer. It was always her aim to have a specific theme in each hymn and this is well demonstrated in 'There are loved ones in the Glory' (Will the circle be unbroken) and 'Jesus Himself drew near'.

"There are loved ones in the glory
Whose dear forms you often miss;
When you close your earthly story
Will you join them in their bliss?

Will the circle be unbroken
By and by, by and by,
In a better home awaiting
In the sky, in the sky?"

The following is based on Luke 24 verse 15 and the record of the Lord's appearance to the two on the road to Emmaus:

"Jesus Himself drew near
And joined them as they walked,
And soon their hearts began to burn,
As of himself He talked:
Draw near, O Lord,
Draw near, O Lord.

ADA RUTH HABERSHON

Jesus Himself drew near,
They were no longer sad;
When He was walking at their side,
How could they but be glad?
Draw near, O Lord,
Draw near, O Lord."

The ministry of song proved a happy service to her, as she believed that the thoughts which formed the subjects of her hymns came in answer to prayer. She could only praise the Lord for what He had given to her through them. She coupled her deep Bible knowledge with a practical prayer life - a combination we could all emulate.

ADA RUTH HABERSHON 1861-1918

"HAD I A THOUSAND TONGUES, I WOULD PRAISE CHRIST JESUS WITH ALL OF THEM."

PETER BOHLER, MORAVIAN PREACHER

Chapter Thirty Seven

JohN GeorgE GovaN
'THE CHIEF' AMONG THE PILGRIMS!

J G Govan came of an illustrious line and could claim as an ancestor Captain William Govan, one-time Royalist but for conscience sake became a Covenanter, who laid down his life for the faith, along with James Guthrie in the Grassmarket, Edinburgh (June 1st 1661). J G's father was also named William, not a soldier but a Glasgow businessman, who stood for the same truths as his forbears. J G was one of a family of six sons and seven daughters, each brought up in the fear and admonition of the Lord.

It was at the age of twelve, when the family were on holiday on the island of Arran, that he was brought to a realisation that he was a sinner and that without Christ he would be forever shut out of God's Heaven. His father was the speaker at one of the Sunday meetings and had posed the question "Will we be gathered together again?" That night the young boy found peace in believing and had that certain knowledge that he would indeed be present for that heavenly re-union.

The influences of early life - the teaching of God's Word and a godly example in the home, the challenge of D L Moody's virile preaching and the spiritual power and enthusiasm of the Salvation

Army - were shaping the young J G. The family were vigorous supporters of all God-honouring evangelistic efforts and their home became an open house. Such impressionable factors stirred the soul of J G.

It was his father's last whispered message to him that was to prove both prophetic and a compelling force to service. He said to him: "You are to be a Witness For Christ." Such a comment had been made by different preachers but the solemnity and sorrow of his father's dying words had a profound impact. J G was involved with a rescue mission in one of the worst parts of Glasgow and he felt he had to devote his whole time to the work of the Kingdom and to sever ties with the family business. He contemplated service on the mission field in India with the Salvationists and also work with the China Inland Mission. However it was in the villages of Scotland that he began missioning on his own account.

The evident blessing of the Lord increased his burden for heathen Scotland. He resolved to ask others to join him, on the basis that they would go out in faith, looking to God alone to supply their needs. In his diary, 14th October 1886, he recorded "the Faith Mission started." Such was the beginning of the organisation which was to spread nationally and internationally, preaching a distinctive message of holiness and full salvation. "Pilgrims" were to campaign in an area for several weeks because as Govan wrote "it is a fight, but we are on the side of victory and our Captain has never been defeated."

The ministry of the new movement was to be advanced by a training college and by the printed page. A magazine "Bright Words for Pilgrims to the Heavenly City" was introduced and the editorship fell to his brother, Horace. The publication contained news, testimonies and reports from the mission fields. Also appearing were occasional poems including 'There's a Saviour from all sin', written by "The Chief" as the Pilgrims affectionately called him. Notice that each verse ends with a significant triumphant shout "Hallelujah!"

Just as his father had befriended Moody and Booth, J G could name many famous preachers as his companions in the work. For example, Campbell Morgan, George Grubb, Andrew Murray and

Dr H Guinness all helped in the early conventions and with training of the Pilgrims. He was also thrilled to be associated with W P Nicholson, whose uncompromising ministry was used of God to turn Ulster from "Civil War to Revival Victory" in the 1920's.

J G completed his pilgrimage in September 1927, as he would have wished "in harness to the last."

"There's a Saviour from all sin;
If you only let Him in
To your heart, He there will reign,
While you trust Him.
He will put the evil out,
Save from every fear and doubt,
And you'll soon begin to shout:
Hallelujah!"

JOHN GEORGE GOVAN 1861-1927

"GOOD HYMNS ARE AN IMMENSE BLESSING TO THE CHURCH OF CHRIST. THERE IS AN ELEVATING, STIRRING, SOOTHING, SPIRITUALISING EFFECT ABOUT A THOROUGHLY GOOD HYMN, WHICH NOTHING ELSE CAN PRODUCE."

J C RYLE

Chapter Thirty Eight

CHARLES SILVESTER HORNE
PREACHER AND POLITICIAN

There were two distinct periods in the life of Silvester Horne. He was the young minister of a fashionable West End church at Kensington, London and in later life the Superintendent of Whitefield's Central Mission and also a Member of Parliament. In his first charge he exercised pulpit propriety with "perfect poise, graceful gesture and voice modulated to express every emotion." At Whitefield's Tabernacle he was freed from such restraints and adopted the methods of the public platform. His passion for preaching burned all the more. The well crafted and eloquent addresses were replaced with direct, personal and practical preaching.

He was a born orator and his early skills were apprenticed as a student in Glasgow University. The power of words was learned at home from his father, who was for some time a Congregational Minister but he resigned the pulpit to become editor of a newspaper owned by his wife's uncle. The evening occupation for the family was to proof read articles for the paper and this was an excellent training in accuracy and correct expression. Thus Silvester became familiar with the printing process and used to set his own compositions, both prose and verse, in type (in those days in individual cast letters). His interest in politics began to develop at this time and this was sustained throughout his life.

Shortly after his sixteenth birthday, he gained an open bursary to Glasgow University. He demonstrated no special brilliance but his diligent studies achieved an Arts degree. His objective was the Congregational ministry and he progressed to Mansfield College, Oxford, to undergo three years of theological training. He first preached for Dr Dale of Birmingham in 1887 on the text "The love of Christ constraineth us." His recognised ability led to a call to the pastorate in Kensington while he was still a student. There he instigated a Children's Guild to encourage young believers and proposed a Forward Movement to promote evangelistic work and to advance Missionary endeavour. He found time to develop his writing talent and produced church histories, a novel and several books on missionary work, preaching and church government. In political circles he was giving expression to his liberal views, especially on the Irish situation. He declared himself a Home Ruler!

As a consequence of his hectic pace of life, he suffered a nervous break-down in 1895. His recourse was to detach himself from his surroundings and interests and set sail for Norway and the Arctic. Refreshed and it seemed fully recovered, he resumed his duties after a short time. However his health deteriorated and again he embarked upon foreign travel. Rather than impose upon the generosity of his congregation, he resigned his pulpit. He journeyed through Switzerland and Italy where "cycling, fresh air and a vegetarian diet" effected a good recovery. By 1897 his church was able to welcome him back once more, and to ease the pressure an assistant was appointed.

When he commenced at Whitefield's he broadened his activities and social, church and political issues went hand in hand. Enjoying freedom from the formal regime experienced at Kensington, he conducted services in the streets of London to reach those who would not or could not come inside a church building. On one such occasion he addressed a crowd from the back of a coal truck. His willingness to do so impressed those who considered themselves unworthy to sit in church with a well-dressed congregation.

In 1909 he was elevated to the office of chairman of the Congregational Union of England and Wales. The following year he campaigned in the General Election and was elected Liberal MP for Ipswich. He was probably the first minister in charge of a church to sit in Parliament since the days of "Praise God" Barebones.

Horne was associated with great men like Dr Dale, J D Jones, Jowett, Campbell Morgan, Theodore Monod and Merle D'Aubigny, but his liberalism in politics ran parallel with liberalism in religion and he became distanced from his early friendships. He defended proposed changes to the Coronation Oath and declared that he did not regard Romanists as idolaters! (Incidentally his son Kenneth was no stranger to controversy - he became a comic actor and for many years had a BBC radio programme called 'Round the Horne' which was often criticised for its subject matter and 'double entendre'.)

In 1914 he was invited to visit the USA to deliver the Yale Lectures on Preaching. These were enthusiastically received and so it was with some sense of satisfaction that he set off with his wife for a well-deserved holiday break in Canada. They sailed from Niagara and it was while they were standing on the deck of the steamer as it entered Toronto, that Silvester Horne fell dead at his wife's feet. Thus, at the early age of 49, was ended his earthly ministry.

Horne had composed a hymn 'Sing we the King who is coming to reign', which gained universal acceptance.

"Sing we the King who is coming to reign,
Glory to Jesus, the Lamb that was slain;
Life and salvation His empire shall bring,
Joy to the nations when Jesus is King.

Come, let us sing praise to our King,
Jesus our King, Jesus our King;
This is our song, who to Jesus belong:
Glory to Jesus, to Jesus our King.

Kingdom of Christ, for Thy coming we pray,
Hasten, O Father, the dawn of the day,
When this new song Thy creation shall sing:
Satan is vanquished, for Jesus is King!"

CHARLES SILVESTER HORNE 1865-1914

Chapter Thirty Nine

Thomas Obadiah Chisholm

THE REPORTER WHO HAD GOOD NEWS TO TELL

I n the middle of the last century there could hardly have been a more rustic birthplace than a log cabin located in the mountains of Kentucky. It was in such a place in the summer of 1866, that our subject first saw the light of day. From this humble beginning, Thomas Obadiah Chisholm was to become a writer, a preacher, a businessman and the author of one of the most popular solos and hymns of the twentieth century.

After completing his own training, he helped out in a mountain-school for a short time. His education sufficiently equipped him to begin work at a weekly newspaper in Franklin County. His days were occupied with seeking out news and stories worthy of public-ation. By the age of twenty-one he had become the associate editor of 'The Franklin Favourite'.

In the course of his work he attended evangelistic meetings with the purpose of writing a report. The preacher was Dr H C Morrison and his text was John 3 verse 3; this was to prove to be the best news the young reporter could ever receive! He came under conviction of sin and was soundly converted! The "new man" dedicated his life to the Lord and on Morrison's advise took a new direction in his career. He transferred his journalistic talents from the secular to the sacred and was appointed the office editor and business manager of the "Pentecostal Herald."

At the same time, he commenced training for the Methodist ministry. He was in due course ordained, but he preferred to work as an evangelist rather than as a pastor. The amount of travel this itinerant ministry involved became a burden to him and his health failed. During his recuperation he decided on yet another new direction. He went into the insurance business as a salesman, in the expectation that the pressures would be less demanding. Alas this was not the case and for many years he alternated between secular employment and evangelistic endeavours.

He kept up his writing throughout this time and his songs were the avenue for expressing Scriptural themes. C Harold Lowden, who coincidentally abandoned a successful position in insurance to become a composer of sacred music, was responsible for progressing Chisholm's reputation as a hymnwriter. He sent a tune to him with the request to add worthwhile words. Taking the experience of Phillippians 1 verse 21, Chisholm wrote-

> "Living for Jesus, a life that is true;
> Trying to please Him in all that I do;
> Yielding allegiance glad-hearted and free;
> This is the pathway of blessing for me."

His hymn 'Great is Thy faithfulness' is without doubt a masterpiece of condensed Scriptural praise. Based on Lamentations 3 verse 23, he developed the theme and highlighted the attributes of God, the testimony of God's creation and the blessings for the believer. Dr William M Runyan's musical setting has well proven to be the perfect partner for his composition. Runyan wrote that this particular poem "held such an appeal that I prayed most earnestly that my tune might carry over its message in a worthy way. The subsequent history of its use, indicates that God answered prayer."

It was not until the 1950's that the hymn gained popularity in the British Isles; this was due in part to the rendition by George Beverly Shea. Chisholm's 'Prodigal Son' was put to music by the composer George C Stebbins and also achieved widespread circulation.

Recurring health problems proved wearisome but the Lord blessed Thomas Chisholm with a long life. Near to the end of his earthly journey, he wrote: "I must not fail to record the unfailing faithfulness of a covenant-keeping God and that He has given me many wonderful displays of His providing care, for which I am filled with astonishing gratefulness."

" 'Great is Thy faithfulness,' O God my Father,
There is no shadow of turning with Thee;
Thou changest not, Thy compassions they fail not;
As Thou hast been Thou for ever wilt be."

THOMAS OBADIAH CHISHOLM 1866-1960

"**P**EOPLE WILL GO ON SINGING UNTIL THE LAST TRUMP BRINGS FORTH THE ANGEL BAND; AND THEN GO ON SINGING INTO THE VERY PRESENCE OF GOD."

HENRY WARD BEECHER, PREACHER

Chapter Forty

HENRY BARRACLOUGH
COMPOSER AND ACCOMPANIST

B y 1914, the International Gospel tour by Dr J Wilbur Chapman and Charles M Alexander had encircled the globe and had reached London. A combination of events led Alexander to our subject. For some twelve years Robert Harkness had been the great singer's pianist but now he felt the time expedient to settle down and go into business in London. (In fact he became a music publisher). Several applicants to replace him had been interviewed but none had Harkness's ability to satisfactorily accompany the Gospel song-music which was peculiarly American.

Alexander had to go beyond the usual avenues of advertisement. His search took him to the London headquarters of the YMCA. When he visited the premises and entered the lounge, there seated at the piano was a "short, stocky young man with dark hair and spectacles, playing a rousing song for a group of men."

This was Henry Barraclough, a young and multi-talented Christian who was employed as a secretary to a Member of Parliament. This audition was enough for Alexander to invite him to travel for a week or two on the Gospel tour of Scotland. "Barrie" gladly consented and spoke of his desire to make use of his musical talent and to give his time more definitely to the Lord's work.

Barraclough's short probation lengthened to several weeks, during which time his natural ability was shaping itself for the special work required. He resigned his employment at Westminster and began a new career as pianist and accompanist. When the mission in Scotland concluded, Alexander returned to the USA, and "Barrie" agreed to sail West to associate himself with the evangelistic endeavours of Chapman and Alexander.

It was in 1915 at the Presbyterian conference at Montreat when the seed was sown for Barraclough to compose the hymn known as 'Ivory Palaces'. Chapman had spoken on the 45th Psalm and particularly referred to verse 8: "All thy garments smell of myrrh, and aloes, and cassia, out of the ivory palaces, whereby they made thee glad." After the service Barraclough thought about the message and the four short phrases of a chorus began to take shape in his mind:

"Out of the ivory palaces
Into a world of woe,
Only His great eternal love
Made my Saviour go."

Then using the outline of Chapman's message he constructed the first three verses. The new composition was sung at the morning session of the conference the next day. Sometime later, at the suggestion of Chapman, the fourth verse was added. He entitled the music 'Montreat'.

"My Lord has garments so wondrous fine,
And myrrh their texture fills;
Its fragrance reached this heart of mine,
With joy my being thrills.

In garments glorious He will come
To open wide the door;
And I shall enter my heavenly home,
To dwell for evermore."

HENRY BARRACLOUGH

He adopted America as his own country and he maintained a ministry in music for almost fifty years in the Presbyterian Church in the USA. The hymn 'Ivory Palaces' gained for him an international reputation but no other composition from his repertoire ever reached its equal.

HENRY BARRACLOUGH BORN 1891

"**B**LESSING, AND HONOUR, AND GLORY, AND POWER BE UNTO HIM THAT SITTETH UPON THE THRONE, AND UNTO THE LAMB FOR EVER AND EVER."

REVELATION C5, V13